J          Scott, Robert Falcon, 1868-1912.
GRAPHY     Scott's last expedition.  From the
ott     personal journals of Captain R. F. Scott.
0.      Foreword by Peter Scott.  2d enl. ed.
924   London, J. Murray, 1964.
          169 p.  illus.  maps.

RELATED
OOKS IN
ATALOG
NDER

1. Antarctic regions. 2. South Pole.
I. Title.                           mj
                                  10830

6

# SCOTT'S LAST EXPEDITION

# SCOTT'S
# LAST EXPEDITION

✤ ✤ ✤

From the Personal Journals of
Captain R. F. Scott, C.V.O., R.N.

✤

Foreword by Peter Scott

JOHN MURRAY

# Note

In some parts of this narrative, passages will be found in inverted commas. These are not parts of Scott's original Journal but additions taken from his private letters.

Passages from Dr Wilson's Journal are enclosed in square brackets and acknowledgment is made to George Seaver's *Edward Wilson of the Antarctic*.

*First published in this edition 1923*
*Twelfth impression 1956*
*Second enlarged edition (with additional*
*extracts from the journals*
*of Capt Scott and Dr Wilson,*
*a foreword by Peter Scott,*
*and additional illustrations) 1964*

*Made and printed in Great Britain*
*for John Murray*
*Fifty Albemarle Street London*
*by William Clowes and Sons Ltd*
*London and Beccles*

# Foreword by Peter Scott

From time to time the reactions of the human spirit in extreme adversity strike the imagination of a whole generation of people, and the story becomes history to be handed down to generations who were not born when the events took place. This seems to have happened to the story of my father's last Antarctic expedition on which he and four companions reached the South Pole, but died of hunger and cold on the way back.

The bare bones of the story are simple enough. In 1910 Captain Scott led his second expedition to the Antarctic with the twofold object of reaching the South Pole for the first time and carrying out an extensive programme of scientific research. He spent the winter at his Base Camp and learned that the famous Norwegian explorer Amundsen, whom he believed to be setting out on a voyage to the Arctic, had changed his plans and was heading for the South Pole. My father refused to prejudice his scientific programme by making a race of the journey to the Pole and stuck to his original time-table. Amundsen, using dog teams, got to the South Pole first, on December 16, 1911. Scott, with Wilson, Oates, Bowers and Evans, on foot and hauling their sledge, arrived on January 17, 1912.

Greatly disappointed at being forestalled, they set off on the 800-mile sledge-haul back to the Base Camp. What happened on that journey turned their story into a legend. How they completed nearly seven-eighths of the distance, how they met abnormal and quite unexpectedly severe weather, how they became frost-bitten, perhaps because of vitamin deficiencies which were little understood in those days, above all how they faced up to these dreadful difficulties, how the glorious Oates walked out to his death to give the others a chance, how they came within 11 miles of a food depôt which could have saved them, and how they finally died in their tent—these were the things which caught the imagination of people all over the world when the story became known.

As they lay in their sleeping-bags, my father and his friends must have found comfort in knowing that the expedition had, in spite of everything, achieved so many of its objects. The organisation of rations and equipment had worked out perfectly to plan. The timing had been upset only by unforeseen and unforseeable weather conditions. The scientists had made their own discoveries, of far more value for the future than mere priority at the Pole. Indeed, the claims of research had always been put first, and were honoured even during the last march. Perhaps their minds dwelt, too, on the fascination and beauty of the Antarctic world, on the habits of penguins, and the splendour of the aurora. Above all, they knew the satisfaction of work well done in one another's faithful company.

'Had we lived,' Scott wrote in a last message to the public, 'I should have had a tale to tell of the hardihood, endurance and courage of my companions that would have stirred the heart of every Englishman. These rough notes and our dead bodies must tell the tale.'

The passage is quoted on the pedestal of the statue made by my mother which stands in Waterloo Place, London. The message, several letters and his diaries—'these rough notes' as he called them—were found when the tent was discovered by a relief party eight months later in the next Antarctic summer.

Captain Scott's diaries have a classic simplicity, yet they form one of the most moving documents in the English language. They can be seen in the British Museum, and extracts from them, and from some of the letters, are reprinted in this book.

More than 50 years have passed since Scott's Last Expedition. There have been two great world wars with their countless examples of courage and self-sacrifice, and in peace time man has sought new adventure in exploration —especially under the sea and in outer space. Yet the story told in Captain Scott's diaries does not date, because it is about the courage of individual people in appalling circumstances. It is as timeless as the human spirit. To read it will never cease to be absorbing and inspiring.

# Contents

# Illustrations

*All photographs, except those otherwise acknowledged,
are the copyright of Paul Popper Ltd., and were
taken by Herbert G. Ponting, F.R.G.S.*

# British Antarctic Expedition 1910

## SHORE PARTIES

ROBERT FALCON SCOTT. *Captain, C.V.O., R.N.*

EDWARD R. G. R. EVANS (Teddy). *Lieutenant, R.N.*

VICTOR L. A. CAMPBELL (The Mate, Mr. Mate). *Lieutenant, R.N.* (*Emergency List*).

HENRY R. BOWERS (Birdie). *Lieutenant, R.I.M.*

LAWRENCE E. G. OATES (Titus, Soldier). *Captain 6th Inniskilling Dragoons.*

G. MURRAY LEVICK (Toffarino, the Old Sport). *Surgeon, R.N.*

EDWARD L. ATKINSON (Jane, Atchison). *Surgeon, R.N., Parasitologist.*

EDWARD ADRIAN WILSON (Bill, Uncle Bill). *B.A., M.B.(Cantab.), Chief of the Scientific Staff, and Zoologist.*

GEORGE C. SIMPSON (Sunny Jim). *D.Sc., Meteorologist.*

T. GRIFFITH TAYLOR (Griff, and Keir Hardie). *B.A., B.Sc., B.E., Geologist.*

EDWARD W. NELSON (Marie, Brontë). *Biologist.*

FRANK DEBENHAM (Deb). *B.A., B.Sc., Geologist.*

CHARLES S. WRIGHT (Silas, Toronto). *B.A., Physicist.*

RAYMOND E. PRIESTLEY (Raymond). *Geologist.*

HERBERT G. PONTING (Ponco). *F.R.G.S., Camera Artist.*

CECIL H. MEARES. *In Charge of Dogs.*

BERNARD C. DAY. *Motor Engineer.*

APSLEY CHERRY-GARRARD (Cherry). *B.A., Asst. Zoologist.*

TRYGGVE GRAN. *Sub-Lieutenant, Norwegian N.R., B.A., Ski Expert.*

W. LASHLY. *Chief Stoker, R.N.*

W. W. ARCHER. *Chief Steward, late R.N.*

THOMAS CLISSOLD. *Cook, late R.N.*

EDGAR EVANS. *Petty Officer, R.N.*

ROBERT FORDE. *Petty Officer, R.N.*

THOMAS CREAN. *Petty Officer, R.N.*

THOMAS S. WILLIAMSON. *Petty Officer, R.N.*

PATRICK KEOHANE. *Petty Officer, R.N.*

GEORGE P. ABBOTT. *Petty Officer, R.N.*

FRANK V. BROWNING. *Petty Officer, 2nd Class, R.N.*

HARRY DICKASON. *Able Seaman, R.N.*

F. J. HOOPER. *Steward, late R.N.*

ANTON OMELCHENKO. *Groom.*
DEMETRI GEROF. *Dog Driver.*

## SHIP'S PARTY

HARRY L. L. PENNELL (Penelope). *Lieutenant, R.N.*
HENRY E. DE P. RENNICK (Parnie). *Lieutenant, R.N.*
WILFRED M. BRUCE. *Lieutenant, R.N.R.*
FRANCIS R. H. DRAKE (Francis). *Asst. Paymaster, R.N. (Retired). Secretary and Meteorologist in Ship.*
DENIS G. LILLIE (Lithley, Hercules). *M.A., Biologist in Ship.*
JAMES R. DENNISTOUN. *In Charge of Mules in Ship.*
ALFRED B. CHEETHAM. *R.N.R., Boatswain.*
WILLIAM WILLIAMS. *Chief Engine-room Artificer, R.N., Engineer.*
WILLIAM A. HORTON. *Engine-room Artificer, 3rd Class, R.N., 2nd Engineer.*
FRANCIS E. C. DAVIES. *Leading Shipwright, R.N.*
FREDERICK PARSONS. *Petty Officer, R.N.*
WILLIAM L. HEALD. *Late P.O., R.N.*
ARTHUR S. BAILEY. *Petty Officer, 2nd Class, R.N.*
ALBERT BALSON. *Leading Seaman, R.N.*
JOSEPH LEESE. *Able Seaman, R.N.*
JOHN HUGH MATHER. *Petty Officer, R.N.V.R.*
ROBERT OLIPHANT. *Able Seaman.*
THOMAS F. MCLEOD. *Able Seaman.*
MORTIMER MCCARTHY. *Able Seaman.*
WILLIAM KNOWLES. *Able Seaman.*
CHARLES WILLIAMS. *Able Seaman.*
JAMES SKELTON. *Able Seaman.*
WILLIAM MCDONALD. *Able Seaman.*
JAMES PATON. *Able Seaman.*
ROBERT BRISSENDEN. *Leading Stoker, R.N.*
EDWARD A. MCKENZIE. *Leading Stoker, R.N*
WILLIAM BURTON. *Leading Stoker, R.N.*
BERNARD J. STONE. *Leading Stoker, R.N.*
ANGUS MCDONALD. *Fireman.*
THOMAS MCGILLON. *Fireman.*
CHARLES LAMMAS. *Fireman.*
W. H. NEALE. *Steward.*

Plan of Hut.

# 1

## Through Stormy Seas

### THE VOYAGE OUT

*Saturday, November 26.*—We advertised our start (from Port Lyttelton) at 3 P.M., and at three minutes to that hour the *Terra Nova* pushed off from the jetty. A great mass of people assembled. K.* and I went out in the ship, but left her inside the heads after passing the *Cambrian*, the only Naval ship present. We came home in the Harbour Tug; two other tugs followed the ship out and innumerable small boats. Ponting busy with cinematograph. We walked over the hills to Sumner. Saw the *Terra Nova*, a little dot to the S.E.

*Monday, November 28.*—Caught 8 o'clock express to Port Chalmers,† Kinsey‡ saw us off. Wilson joined train. Telegram to say *Terra Nova* had arrived Sunday night. Arrived Port Chalmers at 4.30. Found all well.

*Tuesday, November 29.*—To Town Hall to see Mayor. Found all well on board.

We left the wharf at 2.30—bright sunshine—very gay scene. If anything more craft following us than at Lyttelton —Mrs. Wilson, Mrs. Evans, and K. left at Heads and back in Harbour Tug. Other tugs followed farther with Volunteer

* The author's wife.
† Near Dunedin, in the South Island.
‡ Scott's N.Z. friend and agent in Christchurch.

Reserve Gunboat—all left about 4.30. Pennell 'swung'* the ship for compass adjustment, then 'away.'

*Evening.*—Loom of land and Cape Saunders Light blinking.

*Wednesday, November 30.*—Noon 110 miles. Light breeze from northward all day, freshening towards nightfall and turning to N.W. Bright sunshine. Ship pitching with south-westerly swell. All in good spirits except one or two sick.

We are away, sliding easily and smoothly through the water, but burning coal—8 tons in 24 hours reported 8 P.M.

*Thursday, December 1.*—The month opens well on the whole. During the night the wind increased; we worked up to 8, to 9, and to 9·5 knots. Stiff wind from N.W. and confused sea. Awoke to much motion.

The ship a queer and not altogether cheerful sight under the circumstances.

Below one knows all space is packed as tight as human skill can devise—and on deck! Under the forecastle fifteen ponies close side by side, seven one side, eight the other, heads together and groom between—swaying, swaying continually to the plunging irregular, motion.

One takes a look through a hole in the bulkhead and sees a row of heads with sad, patient eyes come swinging up

---

* A mariner's compass points to the magnetic pole if placed clear of any magnetic attraction. Steel vessels, or wooden ships with steel parts or fittings, however, attract the north point of the compass away from the magnetic north pole, but the amount differs according to the direction the vessel heads. From time to time vessels are 'swung'—to ascertain the exact amount of this attraction which is termed the deviation of the compass. This is recorded and allowed for by the navigator at every change of direction of the vessel.

together from the starboard side, whilst those on the port swing back; then up come the port heads, whilst the starboard recede. It seems a terrible ordeal for these poor beasts to stand this day after day for weeks together, and indeed though they continue to feed well the strain quickly drags down their weight and condition; but nevertheless the trial cannot be gauged from human standards. There are horses which never lie down, and all horses can sleep standing; anatomically they possess a ligament in each leg which takes their weight without strain. Even our poor animals will get rest and sleep in spite of the violent motion. Some 4 or 5 tons of fodder and the ever watchful Anton take up the remainder of the forecastle space.

There are four ponies outside the forecastle and to leeward of the fore hatch, and on the whole, perhaps, with shielding tarpaulins, they have a rather better time than their comrades. Just behind the ice-house and on either side of the main hatch are two enormous packing-cases containing motor sledges, each 16 × 5 × 4; mounted as they are several inches above the deck they take a formidable amount of space. A third sledge stands across the break of the poop in the space hitherto occupied by the after winch. All these cases are covered with stout tarpaulin and lashed with heavy chain and rope lashings, so that they may be absolutely secure.

The petrol for these sledges is contained in tins and drums protected in stout wooden packing-cases which are ranged across the deck immediately in front of the poop and abreast the motor sledges. The quantity is $2\frac{1}{2}$ tons and the space occupied considerable.

Round and about these packing-cases, stretching from the galley forward to the wheel aft, the deck is stacked with

BRITISH ANTARCTIC EXPEDITION 1910-13.

coal-bags forming our deck cargo of coal, now rapidly diminishing.

We left Port Chalmers with 462 tons of coal on board, rather a greater quantity than I had hoped for, and yet the load mark was 3 inches above the water. The ship was over 2 feet by the stern,* but this will soon be remedied.

Upon the coal sacks, upon and between the motor sledges, and upon the ice-house are grouped the dogs, thirty-three in all. They must perforce be chained up, and they are given what shelter is afforded on deck, but their position is not enviable. The seas continually break on the weather bulwarks and scatter clouds of heavy spray over the backs of all who must venture into the waist of the ship. The dogs sit with their tails to this invading water, their coats wet and dripping. It is a pathetic attitude, deeply significant of cold and misery; occasionally some poor beast emits a long pathetic whine. Such a life is truly hard for these poor creatures.

We manage somehow to find a seat for every one at our cabin table, although the wardroom contains twenty-four officers. There are generally one or two on watch, which eases matters, but it is a squash. Our meals are simple enough, but it is really remarkable to see the manner in which our two stewards, Hooper and Neald, provide for all requirements—washing up, tidying cabin, and making themselves generally useful in the cheerfullest manner.

With such a large number of hands on board, allowing nine seamen in each watch, the ship is easily worked, and Meares and Oates have their appointed assistants to help them in custody of dogs and ponies, but on such a night as the last with the prospect of dirty weather, the 'after guard'

* *I.e.* below its proper level at that point.

of volunteers is awake and delightfully enthusiastic: some lend a hand if there is difficulty with ponies and dogs, others in shortening or trimming sails, and others again in keeping the bunkers filled with the deck coal.

*Friday, December 2.*—A day of great disaster. From 4 o'clock last night the wind freshened with great rapidity, and very shortly we were under topsails, jib, and staysail* only. It blew very hard and the sea got up at once. Soon we were plunging heavily and taking much water over the lee rail. Oates and Atkinson, with intermittent assistance from others, were busy keeping the ponies on their legs. Cases of petrol, forage, etc., began to break loose on the upper deck; the principal trouble was caused by the loose coal-bags, which were bodily lifted by the seas and swung against the lashed cases. 'You know how carefully everything had been lashed, but no lashings could have withstood the onslaught of these coal-sacks for long'; they acted like battering rams. 'There was nothing for it but to grapple with the evil, and nearly all hands were labouring for hours in the waist of the ship, heaving coal sacks overboard and re-lashing the petrol cases, etc., in the best manner possible under such difficult and dangerous circumstances. The seas were continually breaking over these people and now and again they would be completely submerged. At such times they had to cling for dear life to some fixture to prevent themselves being washed overboard.

'No sooner was some semblance of order restored than some exceptionally heavy wave would tear away the lashing and all the work had to be done again.'

* Topsail, a square sail half-way up the mast; a staysail, one fixed on a stay, or rope supporting a mast; a jib (which is a staysail) stretches from the masthead to the jib-boom or bowsprit.

The night wore on, the sea and wind ever rising, and the ship ever plunging more distractedly; we shortened sail to main topsail and staysail, stopped engines and hove to, but to little purpose. Tales of ponies down came frequently from forward, where Oates and Atkinson laboured through the entire night. Worse was to follow, much worse—a report from the engine-room that the pumps had choked and the water risen over the gratings.

From this moment, about 4 A.M., the water gained in spite of every effort. Lashly, to his neck in rushing water, stuck gamely to the work of clearing suctions. For a time with donkey engine and bilge pump sucking,* it looked as though the water would be got under; but the hope was short lived: five minutes of pumping invariably led to the same result—a general choking of the pumps.

The outlook appeared grim. The amount of water which was being made,† with the ship so roughly handled, was most uncertain. 'We knew that normally the ship was not making much water, but we also knew that a considerable part of the water washing over the upper deck must be finding its way below; the decks were leaking in streams. The ship was very deeply laden; it did not need the addition of much water to get her waterlogged, in which condition anything might have happened.' The hand pump produced only a dribble, and its suction could not be got at; as the water crept higher it got in contact with the boiler and grew warmer—so hot at last that no one could work at the suctions. Williams had to confess he was beaten and must draw fires. What was to be done? Things for the moment

---

* Making a noise which shows that air is being drawn into the pipe.

† A ship 'makes water' when the depth of water in the hold increases.

appeared very black. The sea seemed higher than ever; it came over lee rail and poop, a rush of green water; the ship wallowed in it; a great piece of the bulwark carried clean away. The bilge pump is dependent on the main engine. To use the pump it was necessary to go ahead. It was at such times that the heaviest seas swept in over the lee rail; over and over [again] the rail, from the forerigging to the main, was covered by a solid sheet of water which swept aft and high on the poop. On one occasion I was waist deep when standing on the rail of the poop.

The scene on deck was devastating, and in the engine-room the water, though really not great in quantity, rushed over the floor plates and frames* in a fashion that gave it a fearful significance.

The after guard were organised in two parties by Evans to work buckets; the men were kept steadily going on the choked hand-pumps—this seemed all that could be done for the moment; and what a measure to count as the sole safeguard of the ship from sinking, practically an attempt to bale her out! Yet strange as it may seem the effort has not been wholly fruitless—the string of buckets which has now been kept going for four hours, together with the dribble from the pump, has kept the water under—if anything there is a small decrease.

Meanwhile we have been thinking of a way to get at the suction of the pump: a hole is being made in the engine-room bulkhead, the coal between this and the pump shaft will be removed, and a hole made in the shaft. With so much water coming on board, it is impossible to open the hatch over the shaft. We are not out of the wood, but hope

* Wooden floor boards.

dawns, as indeed it should for me, when I find myself so wonderfully served. Officers and men are singing chanties over their arduous work. Williams is working in sweltering heat behind the boiler to get the door made in the bulkhead. Not a single one has lost his good spirits. A dog was drowned last night, one pony is dead and two others in a bad condition—probably they too will go. 'Occasionally a heavy sea would bear one of them* away, and he was only saved by his chain. Meares with some helpers had constantly to be rescuing these wretched creatures from hanging, and trying to find them better shelter, an almost hopeless task. One poor beast was found hanging when dead; one was washed away with such force that his chain broke and he disappeared overboard; the next wave miraculously washed him on board again, and he is now fit and well.' The gale has exacted heavy toll, but I feel all will be well if we can only cope with the water. Another dog has just been washed overboard. Thank God, the gale is abating. The sea is still mountainously high, but the ship is not labouring so heavily as she was. I pray we may be under sail again before morning.

[*From Dr. Wilson's Journal. Dec. 2.*—It was a weird night's work with the howling gale and the darkness and the immense sea running over the ship every few minutes, and no engines and no sail, and we all in the engine-room black as ink, singing chanties as we passed slopping buckets full of bilge, each man above slopping a little over the heads of all of us below him; wet through to the skin, so much so that some of the party worked altogether naked like Chinese coolies; and the rush of the wave backwards and forwards at the bottom grew hourly less in the dim

* The dogs.

light of a couple of engine-room oil-lamps whose light just made the darkness visible—the ship all the time rolling like a sodden lifeless log, her lee gunwale* under water every time.

... Just about the time when things looked their very worst—the sky was like ink and water was everywhere and everyone was as wet inside their oilskins as the skins were wet without—there came out a most perfect and brilliant rainbow for about half a minute or less and then suddenly and completely went out. If ever there was a moment when such a message was a comfort it was just then; it seemed to remove every shadow of doubt not only as to the present but as to the final issue of the whole expedition. And from that moment matters mended, and everything came all right.]

*Saturday, December 3.*—Yesterday the wind slowly fell towards evening; less water was taken on board, therefore less found its way below, and it soon became evident that our baling was gaining on the engine-room. The work was steadily kept going in two-hour shifts. By 10 P.M. the hole in the engine-room bulkhead was completed, and (Lieut.) Evans, wriggling over the coal, found his way to the pump shaft and down it. He soon cleared the suction 'of the coal balls (a mixture of coal and oil) which choked it,' and to the joy of all a good stream of water came from the pump for the first time. From this moment it was evident we should get over the difficulty, and though the pump choked again on several occasions the water in the engine-room steadily decreased. It was good to visit that spot this morning and to find that the water no longer swished from side to side. In the forenoon fires were laid and lighted—the

* Gunwale—the upper edge of a ship's side.

hand pump was got into complete order and sucked the bilges almost dry, so that great quantities of coal and ashes could be taken out.

Now all is well again, and we are steaming and sailing steadily south within two points of our course. Campbell and Bowers have been busy relisting everything on the upper deck. This afternoon we got out the two dead ponies through the forecastle skylight. It was a curious proceeding, as the space looked quite inadequate for their passage. We looked into the ice-house and found it in the best order.

Though we are not yet safe, as another gale might have disastrous results, it is wonderful to realise the change which has been wrought in our outlook in twenty-four hours. The others have confessed the gravely serious view of our position which they shared with me yesterday, and now we are all hopeful again.

As far as one can gather, besides the damage to the bulwarks of the ship, we have lost two ponies, one dog, '10 tons of coal,' 65 gallons of petrol, and a case of the biologists' spirit—a serious loss enough, but much less than I expected. 'All things considered, we have come off lightly, but it was bad luck to strike a gale at such a time.' The third pony which was down in a sling for some time in the gale is again on his feet. He looks a little shaky, but may pull through if we don't have another gale. Osman, our best sledge dog, was very bad this morning, but has been lying warmly in hay all day, and is now much better. 'Several more were in a very bad way and needed nursing back to life.' The sea and wind seem to be increasing again, and there is a heavy southerly swell, but the glass is high; we ought not to have another gale till it falls.

I would record here a symptom of the spirit which

actuates the men. After the gale the main deck under the forecastle space in which the ponies are stabled leaked badly, and the dirt of the stable leaked through on hammocks and bedding. Not a word has been said; the men living in that part have done their best to fend off the nuisance with oilskins and canvas, but without sign of complaint. Indeed the discomfort throughout the mess deck* has been extreme. Everything has been thrown about, water has found its way down in a dozen places. There is no daylight, and air can come only through the small forehatch; the artificial lamplight has given much trouble. The men have been wetted to the skin repeatedly on deck, and have no chance of drying their clothing. All things considered, their cheerful fortitude is little short of wonderful.

* The living (and dining) room of the ship.

# 2

# In the Pack

*Tuesday, December 13.*—I was up most of the night. Never have I experienced such rapid and complete changes of prospect. Cheetham in the last dog watch* was running the ship through sludgy new ice, making with all sail set four or five knots. Bruce, in the first, took over as we got into heavy ice again; but after a severe tussle got through into better conditions. The ice of yesterday loose with sludgy thin floes between. The middle watch found us making for an open lead,† the ice around hard and heavy. We got through, and by sticking to the open water and then to some recently frozen pools made good progress. At the end of the middle watch trouble began again, and during this and the first part of the morning we were wrestling with the worst conditions we have met. Heavy hummocked bay ice, the floes standing 7 or 8 feet out of water, and very deep below. It was just such ice as we encountered at King Edward's Land in the *Discovery*. I have never seen anything more formidable. The last part of the morning watch was spent in a long recently-frozen lead or pool, and the ship went well ahead again.

These changes sound tame enough, but they are a great strain on one's nerves—one is for ever wondering whether

* To ensure a regular change of duties, the time from 4 to 8 p.m. is divided into two short watches, called dog watches.

† A passage of open water through the icefield.

In the pack—a lead opening up

A berg breaking up in the pack

Mount Erebus with Emperor Penguins in foreground

one has done right in trying to come down so far east, and having regard to coal, what ought to be done under the circumstances.

In the first watch came many alterations of opinion; time and again it looks as though we ought to stop when it seemed futile to be pushing and pushing without result; then would come a stretch of easy going and the impression that all was going very well with us. The fact of the matter is, it is difficult not to imagine the conditions in which one finds oneself to be more extensive than they are. It is wearing to have to face new conditions every hour. This morning we met at breakfast in great spirits; the ship has been boring along well for two hours; then Cheetham suddenly ran her into a belt of the worst and we were held up immediately. We can push back again, I think, but meanwhile we have taken advantage of the conditions to water ship. These big floes are very handy for that purpose at any rate.

We have decided to put fires out and remain here till the conditions change altogether for the better. It is sheer waste of coal to make further attempts to break through as things are at present.

We have been set to the east during the past days; is it the normal set in the region, or due to the prevalence of westerly winds? Possibly much depends on this as concerns our date of release. It is annoying, but one must contain one's soul in patience and hope for a brighter outlook in a day or two. Meanwhile we shall sound, and do as much biological work as is possible.

*Wednesday, December 14.*—One realises the awful monotony of a long stay in the pack, such as Nansen* and others experienced. One can imagine such days as these

* The celebrated Norwegian explorer of the Arctic regions.

lengthening into interminable months and years. For us there is novelty, and every one has work to do or makes work, so that there is no keen sense of impatience.

The current is satisfactory. Both days the observations have been good—it is best that we should go north and west. I had a great fear that we should be drifted east and so away to regions of permanent pack. If we go on in this direction it can only be a question of time before we are freed.

We have all been away on ski on the large floe to which we anchored this morning. Gran is wonderfully good and gives instruction well. It was hot, and garments came off one by one—the Soldier and Atkinson were stripped to the waist eventually, and have been sliding round the floe for some time in that condition. Nearly everyone has been wearing goggles; the glare is very bad. Ponting tried to get a colour picture, but unfortunately the ice colours are too delicate for this.

To-night Campbell, E. Evans, and I went out over the floe, and each in turn towed the other two; it was fairly easy work—that is, to pull 310 to 320 lb. One could pull perhaps more easily on foot, yet it would be impossible to pull such a load on a sledge. What a puzzle this pulling of loads is! If one could think that this captivity was soon to end there would be little reason to regret it; it is giving practice with our deep-sea gear, and has made every one keen to learn the proper use of ski.

*Wednesday, December 21.*—Wilson went over the floe to capture some penguins and lay flat on the surface. We saw the birds run up to him, then turn within a few feet and rush away again. He says that they came towards him when he was singing, and ran away again when he stopped. They were all one-year birds, and seemed exceptionally shy; they appear to be attracted to the ship by a fearful curiosity.

[*From Dr. Wilson's Journal.* Now and again one hears a Penguin cry out in the stillness near at hand or far away, and then perhaps he appears in his dress tail coat and white waistcoat suddenly upon an ice-floe from the water, and catching sight of the ship runs curiously towards her, crying out in his amazement as he comes, from time to time, but only intensifying the wonderful stillness and beauty of the whole fairy-like scene as the glaring sun in the South just touches the horizon and begins again to rise gradually without ever having set at all. We have now broad daylight night and day, but the beauty of the day with its lovely blues and greens amongst the bergs and ice-floes is eclipsed altogether by the marvellous beauty of the midnight, when white ice becomes deepest purple and golden rose and the sky is lemon green without a cloud. No scene in the whole world was ever more beautiful than a clear midnight in the pack.

. . . (The penguins) have lost none of their attractiveness, and are most comical and interesting; as curious as ever, they will always come up at a trot when we sing to them, and you may often see a group of explorers on the poop singing 'For she's got bells on her fingers and rings on her toes, elephants to ride upon wherever she goes,' and so on at the top of their voices to an admiring group of Adélie penguins. Meares is the greatest attraction; he has a full voice which is musical but always very flat. He declares that 'God save the King' will always send them to the water, and certainly it is often successful.]

*Friday, December 23.*—Very little can happen in the personal affairs of our company in this comparatively dull time, but it is good to see the steady progress that proceeds unconsciously in cementing the happy relationship that exists between the members of the party. Never could there have been a greater freedom from quarrels and trouble of all sorts. I have not heard a harsh word or seen a black look. A spirit of tolerance and good humour pervades the whole community, and it is glorious to realise that men can live under conditions of hardship, monotony, and danger in such bountiful good comradeship.

Preparations are now being made for Christmas festivities. It is curious to think that we have already passed the longest day in the southern year.

Saw a whale this morning—estimated 25 to 30 feet. Wilson thinks a new species. Find Adélie penguins in batches of twenty or so. Do not remember having seen so many together in the pack.

*Sunday, December 25, Christmas Day.*—The night before last I had bright hopes that this Christmas Day would see us in open water. The scene is altogether too Christmassy. Ice surrounds us, low nimbus clouds intermittently discharging light snow flakes obscure the sky, here and there small pools of open water throw shafts of black shadow on to the cloud—this black predominates in the direction from whence we have come, elsewhere the white haze of ice reflection is pervading.

We are captured. We do practically nothing under sail to push through, and could do little under steam; and the possibility of advance seems to lessen.

The wind, which has persisted from the west for so long, fell light last night, and to-day comes from the N.E. by N., a steady breeze from 2 to 3 in force.* Since one must have

* The velocity of wind is denoted by numbers (from 1 to 10).

hope, ours is pinned to the possible effect of a continuance of easterly wind. Again the call is for patience and again patience. Here at least we seem to enjoy full security. The ice is so thin that it could not hurt by pressure—there are no bergs within reasonable distance—indeed the thinness of the ice is one of the most tantalising conditions. In spite of the unpropitious prospect every one on board is cheerful and one foresees a merry dinner to-night.

The mess is gaily decorated with our various banners. There was full attendance at the Service this morning and a lusty singing of hymns.

*Midnight*.—A merry evening has just concluded. We had an excellent dinner: tomato soup, penguin breast stewed as an entrée, roast beef, plum pudding and mince pies, asparagus, champagne, port and liqueurs—a festive menu. Dinner began at 6 and ended at 7. For five hours the company has been sitting round the table singing lustily; we haven't much talent, but every one has contributed more or less, 'and the choruses are deafening. It is rather a surprising circumstance that such an unmusical party should be so keen on singing. On Xmas night it was kept up till 1 A.M., and no work is done without a chanty. I don't know if you have ever heard sea chanties being sung. The merchant sailors have quite a collection of them, and invariably call on it when getting up anchor or hoisting sails. Often as not they are sung in a flat and throaty style, but the effect when a number of men break into the chorus is generally inspiriting.'

To-night I noticed a skua gull settle on an upturned block of ice at the edge of a floe on which several penguins were preparing for rest. It is a fact that the latter held a noisy confabulation with the skua as subject—then they advanced as a body towards it; within a few paces the fore-most penguin halted and turned, and then the others pushed him on towards the skua. One after another they jibbed at being first to approach their enemy, and it was only with much chattering and mutual support that they gradually edged towards him.

They couldn't reach him as he was perched on a block, but when they got quite close the skua, who up to that time had appeared quite unconcerned, flapped away a few yards and settled close on the other side of the group of penguins. The latter turned and repeated their former tactics until the skua finally flapped away altogether. It really was extraordinarily interesting to watch the timorous protesting movements of the penguins. The frame of mind producing every action could be so easily imagined and put into human sentiments.

On the other side of the ship part of another group of penguins were quarrelling for the possession of a small pressure block which offered only the most insecure foot-hold. The scrambling antics to secure the point of vantage, the ousting of the bird in possession, and the incontinent loss of balance and position as each bird reached the summit of his ambition was almost as entertaining as the episode of the skua. Truly these little creatures afford much amusement.

*Wednesday, December 28, 1910.*—This morning a number of penguins were diving for food around and under the ship. It is the first time they have come so close to the ship in the pack, and there can be little doubt that the absence of motion of the propeller has made them bold. The Adélie penguin on land or ice is almost wholly ludicrous. Whether sleeping, quarrelling, or playing, whether curious, frightened, or angry, its interest is continuously humorous; but in the water it is another thing: as it darts to and fro a fathom or two below the surface, as it leaps porpoise-like into the air or swims skimmingly over the rippling surface of a pool, it excites nothing but admiration. Its speed probably appears greater than it is, but the ability to twist and turn and the general control of movement is both beautiful and wonderful.

As one looks across the barren stretches of the pack, it is sometimes difficult to realise what teeming life exists immediately beneath its surface.

A tow-net is filled with diatoms* in a very short space of time, showing that the floating plant life is many times richer than that of temperate or tropic seas. These diatoms mostly consist of three or four well-known species. Feeding on these diatoms are countless thousands of small shrimps; they can be seen swimming at the edge of every floe and washing about on the over-turned pieces. In turn they afford food for creatures great and small: the crab-eater or white seal, the penguins, the Antarctic and snowy petrel, and an unknown number of fish.

These fish must be plentiful, as shown by our capture of one on an overturned floe and the report of several seen two days ago by some men leaning over the counter of the ship. These all exclaimed together, and on inquiry all agreed that they had seen half a dozen or more a foot or so in length swimming away under a floe. Seals and penguins capture these fish, as also, doubtless, the skuas and the petrels.

Coming to the larger mammals, one occasionally sees the long lithe sea-leopard,† formidably armed with ferocious teeth and doubtless containing a penguin or two and

* Infinitesimal plants of the seaweed order.
† A species of seal.

perhaps a young crab-eating seal. The killer whale, un-
appeasably voracious, devouring or attempting to devour
every smaller animal, is less common in the pack but
numerous on the coasts. Finally, we have the great browsing
whales of various species, from the vast blue whale, the
largest mammal of all time, to the smaller and less common
bottle-nose and such species as have not yet been named.
Great numbers of these huge animals are seen, and one
realises what a demand they must make on their food supply
and therefore how immense a supply of small sea beasts
these seas must contain. Beneath the placid ice floes and
under the calm water pools the old universal warfare is
raging incessantly in the struggle for existence.

*Friday, December 30.*—We are out of the pack at length
and at last; one breathes again and hopes that it will be
possible to carry out the main part of our programme, but
the coal will need tender nursing.

At six this morning we were well in the open sea, the
sky thick and overcast with occasional patches of fog. We
passed one small berg on the starboard hand with a group
of Antarctic petrels on one side and a group of snow petrels
on the other. It is evident that these birds rely on sea and
swell to cast their food up on ice ledges—only a few find sus-
tenance in the pack where, though food is plentiful, it is not
so easily come by. A flight of Antarctic petrel accompanied
the ship for some distance, wheeling to and fro about her.

'We hold the record for reaching the northern edge of
the pack, whereas three or four times the open Ross Sea*
has been gained at an earlier date.

'I can imagine few things more trying to the patience
than the long wasted days of waiting. Exasperating as it is

* *See* map.

to see the tons of coal melting away with the smallest mileage to our credit, one has at least the satisfaction of active fighting and the hope of better fortune. To wait idly is the worst of conditions. You can imagine how often and how restlessly we climbed to the crow's nest and studied the outlook. And strangely enough there was generally some change to note. A water lead would mysteriously open up a few miles away or the place where it had been would as mysteriously close. Huge icebergs crept silently towards or past us, and continually we were observing these formidable objects with range-finder* and compass to determine the relative movement, sometimes with misgiving as to our ability to clear them. Under steam the change of conditions was even more marked. Sometimes we would enter a lead of open water and proceed for a mile or two without hindrance; sometimes we would come to big sheets of thin ice which broke easily as our iron-shod prow struck them, and sometimes even a thin sheet would resist all our attempts to break it; sometimes we would push big floes with comparative ease and sometimes a small floe would bar our passage with such obstinacy that one would almost believe it possessed of an evil spirit; sometimes we passed through acres of sludgy sodden ice which hissed as it swept along the side, and sometimes the hissing ceased seemingly without rhyme or reason, and we found our screw churning the sea without any effect.

'Thus the steaming days passed away in an ever-changing environment and are remembered as an unceasing struggle.

'The ship behaved splendidly—no other ship, not even the *Discovery*,† would have come through so well. Certainly

---

* A kind of field glass or telescope, for estimating distances.
† Scott's former ship.

the *Nimrod** would never have reached the south water had she been caught in such pack. As a result I have grown strangely attached to the *Terra Nova*. As she bumped the floes with mighty shocks, crushing and grinding a way through some, twisting and turning to avoid others, she seemed a living thing fighting a great fight. If only she had more economical engines she would be suitable in all respects.

'Once or twice we got among floes which stood 7 or 8 feet above water, with hummocks and pinnacles as high as 25 feet. The ship could have stood no chance had such floes pressed against her, and at first we were a little alarmed in such situations. But familiarity breeds contempt; there never was any pressure in the heavy ice, and I'm inclined to think there never would be.

'The weather changed frequently during our journey through the pack. The wind blew strong from the west and from the east; the sky was often darkly overcast; we had snowstorms, flaky snow, and even light rain. In all such circumstances we were better placed in the pack than outside of it. The foulest weather could do us little harm. During quite a large percentage of days, however, we had bright sunshine, which, even with the temperature well below freezing, made everything look bright and cheerful. The sun also brought us wonderful cloud effects, marvellously delicate tints of sky, cloud, and ice, such effects as one might travel far to see. In spite of our impatience we would not willingly have missed many of the beautiful scenes which our sojourn in the pack afforded us.

'Scientifically we have been able to do something. We have managed to get a line of soundings on our route

* Shackleton's ship.

showing the raising of the bottom from the ocean depths to the shallow water on the continental shelf, and the nature of the bottom. With these soundings we have obtained many interesting observations of the temperature of different layers of water in the sea.

'Then we have added a great deal to the knowledge of life in the pack from observation of the whales, seals, penguins, birds, and fishes as well as of the pelagic* beasts which are caught in tow-nets. Life in one form or another is very plentiful in the pack, and the struggle for existence here as elsewhere is a fascinating subject for study.

'We have made a systematic study of the ice also, both the bergs and sea ice, and have got a good deal of useful information concerning it. Also Pennell has done a little magnetic work.

'But of course this slight list of activity in the cause of science is a very poor showing for the time of our numerous experts; many have had to be idle in regard to their own specialities, though none are idle otherwise. All the scientific people keep night watch when they have no special work to do, and I have never seen a party of men so anxious to be doing work or so cheerful in doing it. When there is anything to be done, such as making or shortening sail, digging ice from floes for the water supply, or heaving up the sounding line, it goes without saying that all the afterguard† turn out to do it. There is no hesitation and no distinction. It will be the same when it comes to landing stores or doing any other hard manual labour.

'The spirit of the enterprise is as bright as ever. Every one strives to help every one else, and not a word of com-

* Belonging to the sea (Latin, *pelagus*).
† The more exalted dwellers in the after part of the ship, as contrasted with the sailors in the forecastle.

plaint or anger has been heard on board. The inner life of our small community is very pleasant to think upon and very wonderful considering the extremely small space in which we are confined.

'The attitude of the men is equally worthy of admiration. In the forecastle as in the wardroom there is a rush to be first when work is to be done, and the same desire to sacrifice selfish consideration to the success of the expedition. It is very good to be able to write in such high praise of one's companions, and I feel that the possession of such support ought to ensure success. Fortune would be in a hard mood indeed if it allowed such a combination of knowledge, experience, ability, and enthusiasm to achieve nothing.'

[*From Dr. Wilson's Journal. Off Cape Crozier. Tuesday, January 3.*—. . . Here we brought the ship close in and then we lowered a boat in which were Capt. Scott, Campbell, myself, Cherry-Garrard, Titus* Oates and Taylor. We were to examine the possibilities of landing, but the swell was so heavy in its break amongst the floating blocks of ice along the actual beach and ice-foot that a landing was out of the question. We should have broken up the boat and have all been in the water together. But I assure you it was tantalizing to me, for there, about 6 feet above us, on a small dirty piece of the old bay ice about 10 feet square, one living Emperor Penguin chick was standing disconsolately stranded, and close by it stood one faithful old Emperor Penguin parent asleep. This young Emperor was still in the down, a most interesting fact in the bird's life-history, at which we had rightly guessed, but which no one had actually observed before. It was, however, in a stage never yet seen or collected, for the wings were already

* A nickname, after the hero of the Popish Plot.

quite clean of down and feathered as in the adult; also a line down the breast and part of the head was shed of down. This bird would have been a treasure to me, but we couldn't risk life for it, so it had to remain there with its faithful parent asleep. It was a curious fact that with as much clean ice to live on as they could have wished for, these destitute derelicts of a flourishing colony now gone North on floating bay-ice should have preferred to remain standing on the only piece of bay-ice left—a piece about 10 feet square and now pressed up 6 feet above water-level; evidently wondering why it was so long in starting North with the general exodus which must have taken place just a month ago. The whole incident was most interesting and full of suggestion as to the slow working of the brains of these queer people. Another point was most weird to see, namely, that on the *under* surface of this very dirty piece of sea-ice which was about 2 feet thick, and which hung over the water as a sort of cave, we could see the legs and lower halves of dead Emperor chicks hanging through, and in one place even a dead adult. I hope to make a picture of the whole quaint incident, for it was a corner cram full of Imperial history in the light of what we already knew, and it would otherwise have been about as unintelligible as any group of animate and inanimate nature could possibly have been. As it is, it throws more light on the life history of this strangely primitive bird.

*Jan 4.* . . . These days are with one for all time—they are never to be forgotten—and they are to be found nowhere else in the world but at the poles. The peace of God which passes all understanding reigns here in these days. One only wishes one could bring a glimpse of it away with one with all its unimaginable beauty. . . .]

# 3

# Land

*Wednesday, January 4, 1* A.M.—A group of killer whales was idly diving off the penguin rookery; an old one with a very high straight dorsal fin and several youngsters. We watched a small party of penguins leaping through the water towards their enemies. It seemed impossible that they should have failed to see the sinister fins during their frequent jumps into the air, yet they seemed to take no notice whatever—stranger still, the penguins must have actually crossed the whales, yet there was no commotion whatever, and presently the small birds could be seen leaping away on the other side. One can only suppose the whales are satiated.

*Wednesday, January 4,* P.M.—This work is full of surprises. After many frowns fortune has treated us to the kindest smile—for twenty-four hours we have had a calm with brilliant sunshine. Such weather in such a place comes nearer to satisfying my ideal of perfection than any condition that I ever experienced. The warm glow of the sun with the keen invigorating cold of the air forms a combination which is inexpressibly health-giving and satisfying to me, whilst the golden light on this wonderful scene of mountain and ice satisfies every claim of scenic magnificence. No words of mine can convey the impressiveness of the wonderful panorama displayed to our eyes. Ponting is enraptured and uses expressions which in any one else and alluding to any other subject might be deemed extravagant.

## THE LANDING: A WEEK'S WORK

Whilst we were on shore Campbell was taking the first steps towards landing our stores. Two of the motor sledges were soon hoisted out, and Day with others was quickly unpacking them. Our luck stood again. In spite of all the bad weather and the tons of sea water which had washed over them the sledges and all the accessories appeared as fresh and clean as if they had been packed on the previous day—much credit is due to the officers who protected them with tarpaulins and lashings. After the sledges came the turn of the ponies—there was a good deal of difficulty in getting some of them into the horse box, but Oates rose to the occasion and got most in by persuasion, whilst others were simply lifted in by the sailors. Though all are thin and some few looked pulled down, I was agreeably surprised at the evident vitality which they still possessed—some were even skittish. I cannot express the relief when the whole seventeen were safely picketed on the floe. From the moment of getting on the snow they seemed to take a new lease of life, and I haven't a doubt they will pick up very rapidly. It really is a triumph to have got them through safely and as well as they are. Poor brutes, how they must have enjoyed their first roll, and how glad they must be to have freedom to scratch themselves! It is evident all have suffered from skin irritation—one can imagine the horror of suffering from such an ill for weeks without being able to get at the part that itched. I note that now they are picketed together they administer kindly offices to each other; one sees them gnawing away at each other's flanks in most amicable and obliging manner.

Meares and the dogs were out early, and have been running to and fro most of the day with light loads. The great trouble with them has been due to the fatuous conduct of the penguins. Groups of these have been constantly leaping on to our floe. From the moment of landing on their feet their whole attitude expressed devouring curiosity and a pig-headed disregard for their own safety. They waddle forward, poking their heads to and fro in their usually absurd way, in spite of a string of howling dogs straining to get at them. 'Hulloa!' they seem to say, 'here's a game—what do all you ridiculous things want?' And they come a few steps nearer. The dogs make a rush as far as their leashes or harness allow. The penguins are not daunted in the least, but their ruffs go up and they squawk with semblance of anger, for all the world as though they were rebuking a rude stranger—their attitude might be imagined to convey 'Oh, that's the sort of animal you are; well, you've come to the wrong place—we aren't going to be bluffed and bounced by you,' and then the final fatal steps forward are taken and they come within reach. There is a spring, a squawk, a horrid red patch on the snow, and the incident is closed. Nothing can stop these silly birds. Members of our party rush to head them off, only to be met with evasions—the penguins squawk and duck as much as to say, 'What's it got to do with you, you silly ass? Let us alone.'

With the first spilling of blood the skua gulls assemble, and soon, for them at least, there is a gruesome satisfaction to be reaped. Oddly enough, they don't seem to excite the dogs; they simply alight within a few feet and wait for their

Disembarking the ponies

A skua regurgitating food for her chick

The Castle Berg

turn in the drama, clamouring and quarrelling amongst themselves when the spoils accrue. Such incidents were happening constantly to-day, and seriously demoralising the dog teams. Meares was exasperated again and again.

The motor sledges were running by the afternoon, Day managing one and Nelson the other. In spite of a few minor breakdowns they hauled good loads to the shore. It is early to call them a success, but they are certainly extremely promising.

The next thing to be got out of the ship was the hut, and the large quantity of timber comprising it was got out this afternoon.

And so to-night, with the sun still shining, we look on a very different prospect from that of 48 or even 24 hours ago.

I have just come back from the shore.

The site for the hut is levelled and the erecting party is living on shore in our large green tent with a supply of food for eight days. Nearly all the timber, etc., of the hut is on shore, the remainder half-way there. The ponies are picketed in a line on a convenient snow slope so that they cannot eat sand. Oates and Anton are sleeping ashore to watch over them. The dogs are tied to a long length of chain stretched on the sand; they are coiled up after a long day, looking fitter already. Meares and Demetri are sleeping in the green tent to look after them. A supply of food for ponies and dogs as well as for the men has been landed. Two motor sledges in good working order are safely on the beach.

A fine record for our first day's work. All hands start again at 6 A.M. to-morrow.

It's splendid to see at last the effect of all the months of preparation and organisation. There is much snoring about me as I write (2 P.M.) from men tired after a hard day's work and preparing for such another to-morrow. I also must sleep, for I have had none for 48 hours—but it should be to dream happily.

*Thursday, January 5.*—All hands were up at 5 this morning and at work at 6. Words cannot express the splendid way in which every one works and gradually the work gets organised. I was a little late this morning, and thereby witnessed a most extraordinary scene. Some 6 or 7 killer whales, old and young, were skirting the fast floe edge ahead of the ship; they seemed excited and dived rapidly, almost touching the floe. As we watched, they suddenly appeared astern, raising their snouts out of water. I had heard weird stories of these beasts, but had never associated serious danger with them. Close to the water's edge lay the wire stern rope of the ship, and our two Esquimaux dogs were tethered to this. I did not think of connecting the movements of the whales with this fact, and seeing them so close I shouted to Ponting, who was standing abreast of the ship. He seized his camera and ran towards the floe edge to get a close picture of the beasts, which had momentarily disappeared. The next moment the whole floe under him and the dogs heaved up and split into fragments. One could hear the 'booming' noise as the whales rose under the ice and struck it with their backs. Whale after whale rose under the ice, setting it rocking fiercely; luckily Ponting kept his feet and was able to fly to security. By an extraordinary chance also, the splits had been made around and between the dogs, so that neither of them fell into the water. Then it was clear that the whales shared our astonishment, for one after another their huge hideous heads shot vertically into the air through the cracks which they had made. As they reared them to a height of 6 or 8 feet it was possible to see their tawny head markings, their small glistening eyes, and their terrible array of teeth— by far the largest and most terrifying in the world. There cannot be a doubt that they looked up to see what had happened to Ponting and the dogs.

The latter were horribly frightened and strained to their chains, whining; the head of one killer must certainly have been within 5 feet of one of the dogs.

After this, whether they thought the game insignificant, or whether they missed Ponting, is uncertain, but the terrifying creatures passed on to other hunting grounds, and we were able to rescue the dogs, and what was even more important, our petrol—5 or 6 tons of which were waiting on a piece of ice which was not split away from the main mass.

Of course, we have known well that killer whales continually skirt the edge of the floes and that they would undoubtedly snap up any one who was unfortunate enough to fall into the water; but the facts that they could display such deliberate cunning, that they were able to break ice of such thickness (at least $2\frac{1}{2}$ feet), and that they could act in unison, were a revelation to us. It is clear that they are endowed with singular intelligence, and in future we shall treat that intelligence with every respect.

*Friday, January 6.*—To-day I walked over our peninsula to see what the southern side was like. Hundreds of skuas were nesting and attacked in the usual manner as I passed. They fly round shrieking wildly until they have gained some altitude. They then swoop down with great impetus directly at one's head, lifting again when within a foot of it. The bolder ones actually beat on one's head with their wings as they pass. At first it is alarming, but experience shows that they never strike except with their wings. A skua is nesting on a rock between the ponies and the dogs. People pass every few minutes within a pace or two, yet the old bird has not deserted its chick. In fact, it seems gradually to be getting confidence, for it no longer attempts to swoop at the intruder. To-day Ponting went within a few feet, and by dint of patience managed to get some wonderful cinematograph pictures of its movements in feeding and tending its chick, as well as some photographs of these events at critical times.

*Saturday, January 7.*—We have done splendidly. To-night all the provisions except some in bottles are ashore and nearly all the working paraphernalia of the scientific people—no light item. There remains some hut furniture, 2½ tons of carbide, some bottled stuff, and some odds and ends which should occupy only part of to-morrow; then we come to the two last and heaviest items—coal and horse fodder.

If we are not through in the week we shall be very near it. Meanwhile the ship is able to lie at the ice edge without steam; a splendid saving.

There has been a steady stream of cases passing along the shore route all day and transport arrangements are hourly improving.

Two parties of four and three officers made ten journeys each, covering over 25 miles and dragging loads one way which averaged 250 to 300 lbs. per man.

The ponies are working well now, but beginning to give some excitement. On the whole they are fairly quiet beasts, but they get restive with their loads, mainly but indirectly owing to the smoothness of the ice. They know perfectly well that the swingle trees* and traces are hanging about their hocks and hate it. (I imagine it gives them the nervous feeling that they are going to be carried off their feet.) This makes it hard to start them, and when going they seem to appreciate the fact that the sledges will over-run them should they hesitate or stop. The result is that they are constantly fretful and the more nervous ones tend to become refractory and unmanageable.

Oates is splendid with them—I do not know what we should do without him.

I did seven journeys with ponies and got off with a bump on the head and some scratches.

One pony got away from Debenham close to the ship, and galloped the whole way in with its load behind; the load capsized just off the shore and the animal and sledge dashed into the station. Oates very wisely took this pony straight back for another load.

Two or three ponies got away as they were being harnessed, and careered up the hill again. In fact, there were quite a lot of minor incidents which seemed to endanger life and limb to the animals if not the men, but which all ended safely.

One of Meares' dog teams ran away—one poor dog got turned over at the start and couldn't get up again (Mukàka). He was dragged at a gallop for nearly half a mile; I gave him up as dead, but apparently he was very little hurt.

The ponies are certainly going to keep things lively as time goes on and they get fresher. Even as it is, their

* Crossbars on a pivot, to the ends of which the traces are tied for pulling.

condition can't be half as bad as we imagined; the runaway pony wasn't much done even after the extra trip.

The station is beginning to assume the appearance of an orderly camp. We continue to find advantages in the situation; the long level beach has enabled Bowers to arrange his stores in the most systematic manner. Everything will be handy and there will never be a doubt as to the position of a case when it is wanted. The hut is advancing apace—already the matchboarding is being put on. The framework is being clothed. It should be extraordinarily warm and comfortable, for in addition to this double coating of insulation, dry seaweed in quilted sacking, I propose to stack the pony fodder all around it.

I am wondering how we shall stable the ponies in the winter.

The only drawback to the present position is that the ice is getting thin and sludgy in the cracks and on some of the floes. The ponies drop their feet through, but most of them have evidently been accustomed to something of the sort; they make no fuss about it. Everything points to the desirability of the haste which we are making—so we go on to-morrow, Sunday.

A whole host of minor ills besides snow blindness have come upon us. Sore faces and lips, blistered feet, cuts and scratches; there are few without some troublesome ailment, but, of course, such things are 'part of the business.' The soles of my feet are terribly sore.

'Of course the elements are going to be troublesome, but it is good to know them as the only adversary and to feel there is so small a chance of internal friction.'

Ponting had an alarming adventure about this time. Bent on getting artistic photographs with striking objects, such as hummocked floes or reflecting water, in the foreground, he used to depart with his own small sledge laden with cameras and cinematograph to journey alone to the grounded icebergs. One morning as he tramped along harnessed to his sledge, his snow glasses clouded with the mist of perspiration, he suddenly felt the ice giving under his feet. He describes the sensation as the worst he ever experienced, and one can well believe it; there was no one near to have lent assistance had he gone through. Instinctively he plunged forward, the ice giving at every step and the sledge dragging through water. Providentially the weak area he had struck was very limited, and in a minute or two he pulled out on a firm surface. He remarked that he was perspiring very freely!

# 4

## Settling in

*Tuesday, January 10.*—We have been six days in McMurdo Sound and to-night I can say we are landed. Were it impossible to land another pound we could go on without hitch. Nothing like it has been done before; nothing so expeditious and complete. This morning the main loads were fodder. Sledge after sledge brought the bales, and early in the afternoon the last (except for about a ton stowed with Eastern Party stores) was brought on shore. Some addition to our patent fuel was made in the morning, and later in the afternoon it came in a steady stream. We have more than 12 tons and could make this do if necessity arose.

In addition to this, oddments have been arriving all day—instruments, clothing, and personal effects. Our camp is becoming so perfect in its appointments that I am almost suspicious of some drawback hidden by the summer weather.

The hut is progressing apace, and all agree that it should be the most perfectly comfortable habitation. 'It amply repays the time and attention given to the planning.' The sides have double boarding inside and outside the frames, with a layer of our excellent quilted seaweed insulation between each pair of boardings. The roof has a single matchboarding* inside, but on the outside is a matchboarding, then a layer of 2-ply 'ruberoid,' then a layer of quilted

* Thin boards, fitting close together.

seaweed, then a second matchboarding, and finally a cover of 3-ply 'ruberoid.' The first floor is laid, but over this there will be a quilting, a felt layer, a second boarding, and finally linoleum; as the plenteous volcanic sand can be piled well up on every side it is impossible to imagine that draughts can penetrate into the hut from beneath, and it is equally impossible to imagine great loss of heat by contact or radiation in that direction. To add to the wall insulation the south and east sides of the hut are piled high with compressed-forage bales, whilst the north side is being prepared as a winter stable for the ponies. The stable will stand between the wall of the hut and a wall built of forage bales, six bales high and two bales thick. This will be roofed with rafters and tarpaulin, as we cannot find enough boarding. We shall have to take care that too much snow does not collect on the roof, otherwise the place should do excellently well.

Some of the ponies are very troublesome, but all except two have been running to-day, and until this evening there were no excitements. After tea Oates suggested leading out the two intractable animals behind other sledges; at the same time he brought out the strong, nervous grey pony. I led one of the supposedly safe ponies, and all went well whilst we made our journey; three loads were safely brought in. But whilst one of the sledges was being unpacked the pony tied to it suddenly got scared. Away he dashed with sledge attached; he made straight for the other ponies, but finding the incubus still fast to him he went in wider circles, galloped over hills and boulders, narrowly missing Ponting and his camera, and finally dashed down hill to camp again pretty exhausted—oddly enough, neither sledge nor pony was much damaged. Then we departed again in the same order. Half-way over the floe my rear pony got his foreleg foul of his halter, then got frightened, tugged at his halter, and lifted the unladen sledge to which he was tied—then the halter broke and away he went. But by this time the damage was done. My pony snorted wildly and sprang forward as the sledge banged to the ground. I just managed to hold him till Oates came up, then we started again; but he was thoroughly frightened—all my blandishments failed when he reared and plunged a second time, and I was obliged to let go. He galloped back and the party dejectedly returned. At the camp P.O. Evans got hold of the pony, but in a moment it was off again, knocking Evans off his legs. Finally he was captured and led forth once more between Oates and Anton. He remained fairly well on the outward journey, but on the homeward grew restive again; Evans, who was now leading him, called for Anton, and both tried to hold him, but to no purpose—he dashed off, upset his load, and came back to camp with the sledge. All these troubles arose after he had made three journeys without a hitch and we had come to regard him as a nice, placid, gritty pony. Now I'm afraid it will take a deal of trouble to get him safe again, and we have three very troublesome beasts instead of two. I have written this in some detail to show the unexpected difficulties that arise with these animals, and the impossibility of knowing exactly where one stands. The majority of our animals seem pretty quiet now, but any one of them may break out in this way if things go awry. There is no doubt that the bumping of the sledges close at the heels of the animals is the root of the evil.

The weather has the appearance of breaking. We had a strongish northerly breeze at midday with snow and hail storms, and now the wind has turned to the south and the sky is overcast with threatenings of a blizzard. The floe is cracking and pieces may go out—if so the ship will have to get up steam again. The hail at noon made the surface very bad for some hours; the men and dogs felt it most.

The dogs are going well, but Meares says he thinks that several are suffering from snow blindness. I never knew a dog get it before, but Day says that Shackleton's dogs suffered from it.

*Thursday, January 12.*—Sledging began as usual this morning; seven ponies and the dog teams were hard at it all the forenoon. I ran six journeys with five dogs, driving them in the Siberian fashion for the first time. It was not difficult, but I kept forgetting the Russian words at critical moments: 'Ki'—'right'; 'Tchuri'—'left'; 'Itah'—'right ahead'; [here is a blank in memory and in Diary]—'get along'; 'Paw'—'stop.' Even my short experience makes me think that we may have to reorganise this driving. I am inclined for smaller teams and the driver behind the sledge. However, it's early days to decide such matters, and we shall learn much on the depôt journey.*

Early in the afternoon a message came from the ship to say that all stores had been landed. Nothing remains to be brought but mutton, books and pictures, and the pianola. So at last we really are a self-contained party ready for all emergencies. We are LANDED eight days after our arrival— a very good record.

The hut could be inhabited at this moment, but probably we shall not begin to live in it for a week.

* The journey to establish depôts at which the main expedition could refit and get supplies. The party left a fortnight after this date.

*Sunday, January 15.*—We had decided to observe this day as a 'day of rest,' and so it has been.

At one time or another the majority have employed their spare hours in writing letters.

We rose late, having breakfast at nine. The morning promised well and the day fulfilled the promise: we had bright sunshine and practically no wind.

At 10 A.M. the men and officers streamed over from the ship, and we all assembled on the beach and I read Divine Service, our first Service at the camp and impressive in the open air. After Service I told Campbell that I should have to cancel his two ponies and give him two others. He took it like the gentleman he is, thoroughly appreciating the reason.

He had asked me previously to be allowed to go to Cape Royds over the glacier and I had given permission. After our talk we went together to explore the route, which we expected to find much crevassed. I intended to go only a short way, but on reaching the snow above the uncovered hills of our Cape I found the surface so promising and so free from cracks that I went quite a long way.* Eventually I turned, leaving Campbell, Gran, and Nelson roped together and on ski to make their way onward, but not before I felt certain that the route to Cape Royds would be quite easy. As we topped the last rise we saw Taylor and Wright some way ahead on the slope; they had come up by a different route. Evidently they are bound for the same goal.

I returned to camp, and after lunch Meares and I took a sledge and nine dogs over the Cape to the sea ice on the south side and started for Hut Point.† We took a little

* This tour was over the left (E.) shore of McMurdo Sound.

† Near Cape Armitage, on the edge of the barrier, at the point where the ice-field begins to be permanent.

provision and a cooker and our sleeping-bags. Meares had found a way over the Cape which was on snow all the way except about 100 yards. The dogs pulled well, and we went towards the Glacier Tongue at a brisk pace; found much of the ice uncovered. Towards the Glacier Tongue there were some heaps of snow much wind-blown. As we rose the glacier we saw the *Nimrod* depôt some way to the right and made for it. We found a good deal of compressed fodder and boxes of maize, but no grain crusher as expected. The open water was practically up to the Glacier Tongue.

We descended by an easy slope ¼ mile from the end of the Glacier Tongue, but found ourselves cut off by an open crack some 15 feet across and had to get on the glacier again and go some ½ mile farther in. We came to a second crack, but avoided it by skirting to the west. From this point we had an easy run without difficulty to Hut Point. There was a small pool of open water and a longish crack off Hut Point. I got my feet very wet crossing the latter. We passed hundreds of seals at the various cracks.

On arrival at the hut, to my annoyance we found it filled with snow. Shackleton reported that the door had been forced by the wind, but that he had made an entrance by the window and found shelter inside—other members of his party used it for shelter. But they actually went away and left the window (which they had forced) open; as a result, nearly the whole of the interior of the hut is filled with hard icy snow, and it is now impossible to find shelter inside.

Meares and I were able to clamber over the snow to some extent and to examine the neat pile of cases in the middle, but they will take much digging out. We got some asbestos sheeting from the magnetic hut and made the best shelter we could to boil our cocoa.

There was something too depressing in finding the old hut in such a desolate condition. I had had so much interest in seeing all the old landmarks and the huts apparently intact. To camp outside and feel that all the old comfort and cheer had departed, was dreadfully heartrending. I went to bed thoroughly depressed. It seems a fundamental expression of civilised human sentiment that men who come to such places as this should leave what comfort they can to welcome those who follow, and finding that such a simple duty had been neglected by our immediate predecessors oppressed me horribly.

[*From Dr. Wilson's Journal. January 14.*—He (Scott) also told me the plans for our depôt journey on which we shall be starting in about ten days' time. He wants me to be a dog driver with himself, Meares and Teddie Evans, and this is what I would have chosen had I had a free choice. . . . The dogs run in two teams and each team wants two men. It means a lot of running as they are being driven now, but it is the fastest and most interesting work of all, and we go ahead of the whole caravan with lighter loads and at a faster rate; moreover, if any traction except ourselves can reach the top of Beardmore Glacier, it will be the dogs, and the dog drivers are therefore the people who will have the best chance of doing the top piece of the ice cap at 10,000 feet to the Pole. May I be there! About this time next year may I be there or thereabouts!* With so many young bloods in the heyday of youth and strength beyond my own I feel there will be a most difficult task in making choice towards the end and a most keen competition—*and*

* That is, on the final journey to the Pole.

a universal lack of selfishness and self-seeking with a complete absence of any jealous feeling in any single one of the comparatively large number who at present stand a chance of being on the last piece next summer.

It will be an exciting time, and the excitement has already begun in the healthiest possible manner. I have never been thrown in with a more unselfish lot of men— each one doing his utmost fair and square in the most cheery manner possible.]

*Tuesday, January 17.*—We took up our abode in the hut to-day and are simply overwhelmed with its comfort. After breakfast this morning I found Bowers making cubicles as I had arranged, but I soon saw these would not fit in, so instructed him to build a bulkhead of cases which shuts off the officers' space from the men's, I am quite sure to the satisfaction of both. The space between my bulkhead and the men's I allotted to five: Bowers, Oates, Atkinson, Meares, and Cherry-Garrard. These five are all special friends and have already made their dormitory very habitable. Simpson and Wright are near the instruments in their corner. Next come Day and Nelson in a space which includes the latter's 'Lab.' near the big window; next to this is a space for three—Debenham, Taylor, and Gran; they also have already made their space part dormitory and part workshop.

It is fine to see the way every one sets to work to put things straight; in a day or two the hut will become the most comfortable of houses, and in a week or so the whole station, instruments, routine, men and animals, etc., will be in working order.

It is really wonderful to realise the amount of work which has been got through of late.

It will be *a fortnight to-morrow* since we arrived in McMurdo Sound, and here we are absolutely settled down and ready to start on our depôt journey directly the ponies have had a proper chance to recover from the effects of the voyage. I had no idea we should be so expeditious.

It snowed hard all last night; there were about three or four inches of soft snow over the camp this morning and Simpson tells me some six inches out by the ship. The camp looks very white. During the day it has been blowing very hard from the south, with a great deal of drift. Here in this camp as usual we do not feel it much, but we see the anemometer racing on the hill and the snow clouds sweeping past the ship. The floe is breaking between the point and the ship, though curiously it remains fast on a direct route to the ship. Now the open water runs parallel to our ship road and only a few hundred yards south of it. Yesterday, the whaler was rowed in close to the camp, and if the ship had steam up she could steam round to within a few hundred yards of us. The big wedge of ice to which the ship is holding on the outskirts of the Bay can have very little grip to keep it in and must inevitably go out very soon. I hope this may result in the ship finding a more sheltered and secure position close to us.

A big iceberg sailed past the ship this afternoon. Atkinson declares it was the end of the Cape Barne Glacier. I hope they will know in the ship, as it would be interesting to witness the birth of a glacier in this region.

It is clearing to-night, but still blowing hard. The ponies don't like the wind, but they are all standing the cold wonderfully and all their sores are healed up.

*Thursday, January 19.*—The hut is becoming the most comfortable dwelling-place imaginable. We have made

Adélie penguins courting

The tenements. (Cherry-Garrard, Bowers, Oates, Meares, Atkinson)

Scott in his 'den', writing up his Journal

unto ourselves a truly seductive home, within the walls of which peace, quiet, and comfort reign supreme.

Such a noble dwelling transcends the word 'hut,' and we pause to give it a more fitting title only from lack of the appropriate suggestion. What shall we call it?

'The word "hut" is misleading. Our residence is really a house of considerable size, in every respect the finest that has ever been erected in the Polar regions; 50 ft. long by 25 wide and 9 ft. to the eaves.

'If you can picture our house nestling below this small hill on a long stretch of black sand, with many tons of provision cases ranged in neat blocks in front of it and the sea lapping the ice-foot below, you will have some idea of our immediate vicinity. As for our wider surroundings it would be difficult to describe their beauty in sufficiently glowing terms. Cape Evans is one of the many spurs of Erebus and the one that stands closest under the mountain, so that always towering above us we have the grand snowy peak with its smoking summit. North and south of us are deep bays, beyond which great glaciers come rippling over the lower slopes to thrust high blue-walled snouts into the sea. The sea is blue before us, dotted with shining bergs or ice floes, whilst far over the Sound, yet so bold and magnificent as to appear near, stand the beautiful Western Mountains with their numerous lofty peaks, their deep glacial valley and clear cut scarps, a vision of mountain scenery that can have few rivals.

'Ponting is the most delighted of men; he declares this is the most beautiful spot he has ever seen, and spends all day and most of the night in what he calls "gathering it in" with camera and cinematograph.'

The wind has been boisterous all day, to advantage after

5

the last snow fall, as it has been drifting the loose snow along and hardening the surfaces. The horses don't like it, naturally, but it wouldn't do to pamper them so soon before our journey. I think the hardening process must be good for animals though not for men; nature replies to it in the former by growing a thick coat with wonderful promptitude. It seems to me that the shaggy coats of our ponies are already improving. The dogs seem to feel the cold little so far, but they are not so exposed.

A milder situation might be found for the ponies if only we could picket them off the snow.

Bowers has completed his southern storeroom and brought the wing across the porch on the windward side, connecting the roofing with that of the porch. The improvement is enormous and will make the greatest difference to those who dwell near the door.

The carpenter has been setting up standards and roof beams for the stables, which will be completed in a few days.

This morning I overhauled all the fur sleeping-bags and found them in splendid order—on the whole the skins are excellent. Since that I have been trying to work out sledge details, but my head doesn't seem half as clear on the subject as it ought to be.

I have fixed the 25th as the date for our departure. P.O. Evans is to get all the sledges and gear ready whilst Bowers superintends the filling of provision bags.

Griffith Taylor and his companions have been seeking advice as to their Western trip.* Wilson, dear chap, has been doing his best to coach them.

Ponting has fitted up his dark-room—doing the carpenter-

* A three months' tour of inspection (mainly geological) from the Ferrar Glacier (*see* Map) in the early part of 1911.

ing work with extraordinary speed and to every one's admiration. To-night he made a window in the dark-room in an hour or so.

Meares has become enamoured of the gramophone. We find we have a splendid selection of records. The pianola is being brought in sections, but I'm not at all sure it will be worth the trouble. Oates goes steadily on with the ponies—he is perfectly excellent and untiring in his devotion to the animals.

Day and Nelson, having given much thought to the proper fitting up of their corner, have now begun work. There seems to be little doubt that these ingenious people will make the most of their space.

I have done quite a lot of thinking over the autumn journeys and much remains to be done, mainly on account of the prospect of being cut off from our winter quarters; for this reason we must have a great deal of food for animals and men.

*Friday, January 20.*—Our house has assumed great proportions. Bowers' annexe is finished, roof and all thoroughly snow-tight; an excellent place for spare clothing, furs, and ready use stores, and its extension affording complete protection to the entrance porch of the hut. The stables are nearly finished—a thoroughly stout, well-roofed lean-to on the north side. Nelson has a small extension on the east side and Simpson a pre-arranged projection on the S.E. corner, so that on all sides the main building has thrown out limbs. Simpson has almost completed his ice cavern, light-tight lining, niches, floor and all. Wright and Forde have almost completed the absolute hut, a patchwork building for which the framework only was brought—but it will be very well adapted for our needs.

Gran has been putting 'record' on the ski runners. Record is a mixture of vegetable tar, paraffin, soft soap, and linseed oil, with some patent addition which prevents freezing—according to Gran.

P.O. Evans and Crean have been preparing sledges; Evans shows himself wonderfully capable, and I haven't a doubt as to the working of the sledges he has fitted up.

We have been serving out some sledging gear and wintering boots. We are delighted with everything. First the felt boots and felt slippers made by Jaeger and then summer wind clothes and fur mits—nothing could be better than these articles. Finally to-night we have overhauled and served out two pairs of finnesko (fur boots) to each traveller. They are excellent in quality. At first I thought they seemed small, but a stiffness due to cold and dryness misled me—a little stretching and all was well. They are very good indeed. I have an idea to use putties to secure our wind trousers to the finnesko. But indeed the whole time we are thinking of devices to make our travelling work easier.

'We have now tried most of our stores, and so far we have not found a single article that is not perfectly excellent in quality and preservation. We are well repaid for all the trouble which was taken in selecting the food list and the firms from which the various articles could best be obtained, and we are showering blessings on Mr. Wyatt's* head for so strictly safeguarding our interests in these particulars.

'Our clothing is as good as good. In fact, first and last, running through the whole extent of our outfit, I can say with some pride that there is not a single arrangement which I would have had altered.'

* Business manager of the expedition.

The pianola has been erected by Rennick. He is a good fellow. The pianola has been his special care, and it shows well that he should give so much pains in putting it right for us.

Day has been explaining the manner in which he hopes to be able to cope with the motor sledge difficulty. He is hopeful of getting things right, but I fear it won't do to place more reliance on the machines.

Everything looks hopeful for the depôt journey if only we can get our stores and ponies past the Glacier Tongue.

We had some seal rissoles to-day so extraordinarily well cooked that it was impossible to distinguish them from the best beef rissoles. I told two of the party they were beef, and they made no comment till I enlightened them after they had eaten two each. It is the first time I have tasted seal without being aware of its particular flavour. But even its own flavour is acceptable in our cook's hands—he really is excellent.

[*From Dr Wilson's Journal. January 29.*—The seals have been giving a lot of trouble, that is just to Meares and myself with our dogs. The whole teams go absolutely crazy when they sight them or get wind of them, and there are literally hundreds along some of the cracks. Occasionally when one pictures oneself quite away from trouble of that kind, an old seal will pop his head up at a blowhole a few yards ahead of the team, and they are all on top of him before one can say 'Knife!' Then one has to rush in with the whip—and every one of the team of eleven jumps over the harness of the dog next to him and the harnesses become a muddle that takes much patience to unravel, not to mention care lest the whole team should get away with the sledge and its load and leave one behind to follow on foot at leisure. I never did get left the whole of this journey, but I was often very near it and several times had only time to seize a strap or a part of the sledge and be dragged along helter-skelter over everything that came in the way till the team got sick of galloping and one could struggle to one's feet again. One gets very wary and wide awake when one has to manage a team of eleven dogs and a sledge load by oneself, but it was a most interesting experience, and I had a delightful leader, 'Stareek' by name—Russian for 'Old Man,' and he was the most wise old man. We have to use Russian terms with all our dogs. 'Ki Ki' means go to the right, 'Chui' means go to the left, 'Esh to' means lie down—and the remainder are mostly swear words which mean everything else which one has to say to a dog team.

Dog driving like this in the orthodox manner is a very different thing to the beastly dog driving we perpetrated in the *Discovery* days. I got to love all my team and they got to know me well, and my old leader even now, six months after I have had anything to do with him,* never fails to come and speak to me whenever he sees me, and he knows me and my voice ever so far off. He is quite a ridiculous 'old man' and quite the nicest, quietest, cleverest old dog I have ever come across. He looks in face as if he knew all the wickedness of the world and all its cares and as if he were bored to death by them.]

* Presumably Dr Wilson read over his Journal and added to it during the following winter in the Hut.

# The Depôt Laying Expedition*

*Thursday, February 2.*—IMPRESSIONS

The seductive folds of the sleeping-bag.

The hiss of the primus and the fragrant steam of the cooker issuing from the tent ventilator.

The small green tent and the great white road.

The whine of a dog and the neigh of our steeds.

The driving cloud of powdered snow.

The crunch of footsteps which break the surface crust.

The wind-blown furrows.

The blue arch beneath the smoky cloud.

The crisp ring of the ponies' hoofs and the swish of the following sledge.

The droning conversation of the march as driver encourages or chides his horse.

The patter of dog pads.

The gentle flutter of our canvas shelter.

Its deep booming sound under the full force of a blizzard.

The drift snow like finest flour penetrating every hole and corner—flickering up beneath one's head covering, pricking sharply as a sand blast.

The sun with blurred image peeping shyly through the wreathing drift giving pale shadowless light.

The eternal silence of the great white desert. Cloudy

* This established depôts as far south as One-Ton Depôt, for the expedition of next year.

columns of snow drift advancing from the south, pale yellow wraiths, heralding the coming storm, blotting out one by one the sharp-cut lines of the land.

The blizzard—Nature's protest—the crevasse, Nature's pitfall—that grim trap for the unwary—no hunter could conceal his snare so perfectly—the light rippled snow bridge gives no hint or sign of the hidden danger, its position unguessable till man or beast is floundering, clawing and struggling for foothold on the brink.

The vast silence broken only by the mellow sounds of the marching column.

*Saturday, February 4.*—. . . A dog must be either eating, asleep, or *interested*. His eagerness to snatch at interest, to chain his attention to something, is almost pathetic. The monotony of marching kills him.

This is the fearfullest difficulty for the dog driver on a snow plain without leading marks or objects in sight. The dog is almost human in its demand for living interest, yet fatally less than human in its inability to foresee.

The dog lives for the day, the hour, even the moment. The human being can live and support discomfort for a future.


A SKETCH OF THE LIFE AT HUT POINT*

*April 7th.*—We gather around the fire seated on packing-cases, with a hunk of bread and butter and a steaming pannikin of tea, and life is well worth living. After lunch

---

* This was Discovery Hut (see Plan, f.p. 1) now made habitable, to which the Depôt Laying party returned, and where—with another party from the north—they waited for the sea to freeze before return-ing to the Hut at Cape Evans. It was on arrival at Discovery Hut that they first received news of Amundsen's expedition.

we are out and about again; there is little to tempt a long stay indoors, and exercise keeps us all the fitter.

The failing light and approach of supper drive us home again with good appetites about 5 or 6 o'clock, and then the cooks rival one another in preparing appetising dishes of fried seal liver. A single dish may not seem to offer much opportunity of variation, but a lot can be done with a little flour, a handful of raisins, a spoonful of curry powder, or the addition of a little boiled pea meal. Be this as it may, we never tire of our dish, and exclamations of satisfaction can be heard every night—or nearly every night; for two nights ago [April 4] Wilson, who has proved a genius in the invention of 'plats,*' almost ruined his reputation. He proposed to fry the seal liver in penguin blubber, suggesting that the latter could be freed from all rankness. The blubber was obtained and melted down with great care, the result appeared as delightfully pure fat free from smell; but appearances were deceptive; the 'fry' proved redolent of penguin, a concentrated essence of that peculiar flavour which faintly lingers in the meat and should not be empha-sised. Three heroes got through their pannikins, but the rest of us decided to be contented with cocoa and biscuit after tasting the first mouthful. After supper we have an hour or so of smoking and conversation—a cheering, pleasant hour—in which reminiscences are exchanged by a company which has very literally had world-wide experience. There is scarce a country under the sun which one or another of us has not travelled in, so diverse are our origins and occupations. An hour or so after supper we tail off one by one, spread out our sleeping-bags, take off our shoes and creep into comfort, for our reindeer bags

* From the French; a dish (of food).

are really warm and comfortable now that they have had a chance of drying, and the hut retains some of the heat generated in it. Thanks to the success of the blubber lamps and to a fair supply of candles, we can muster ample light to read for another hour or two, and so tucked up in our furs we study the social and political questions of the past decade.

We muster no less than sixteen. Seven of us pretty well cover the floor of one wing of the L-shaped enclosure, four sleep in the other wing, which also holds the store, whilst the remaining five occupy the annexe and affect to find the colder temperature more salubrious. Every one can manage eight or nine hours' sleep without a break, and not a few would have little difficulty in sleeping the clock round, which goes to show that our extremely simple life is an exceedingly healthy one, though with faces and hands blackened with smoke, appearances might not lead an outsider to suppose it.

# 6

# Home Impressions

ON RETURNING TO THE HUT, APRIL 13, 1911

AFTER our primitive life at Cape Armitage* it was wonderful to enter the precincts of our warm, dry Cape Evans home. The interior space seemed palatial, the light resplendent, and the comfort luxurious. It was very good to eat in civilised fashion, to enjoy the first bath for three months, and have contact with clean, dry clothing. Such fleeting hours of comfort (for custom soon banished their delight) are the treasured remembrance of every Polar traveller. They throw into sharpest contrast the hardships of the past and the comforts of the present, and for the time he revels in the unaccustomed physical contentment that results.

I was not many hours or even minutes in the hut before I was dragged round to observe in detail the transformation which had taken place during my absence, and in which a very proper pride was taken by those who had wrought it.

Simpson's Corner† was the first visited. Here the eye travelled over numerous shelves laden with a profusion of self-recording instruments, electric batteries and switch-boards, whilst the ear caught the ticking of many clocks, the gentle whirr of a motor, and occasionally the trembling note of an electric bell. But such sights and sounds conveyed

* Temporary quarters, *see Map*.
† *See* Plan f.p. 1.

only an impression of the delicate methodical means by which the daily and hourly variations of our weather conditions were being recorded—a mere glimpse of the intricate arrangements of a first-class meteorological station—the one and only station of that order which has been established in Polar regions. It took me days and even months to realise fully the aims of our meteorologist and the scientific accuracy with which he was achieving them. The first impression, which I am here describing, was more confused; I appreciated only that by going to 'Simpson's Corner' one could ascertain at a glance how hard the wind was blowing and had been blowing, how the barometer was varying, to what degree of cold the thermometer had descended; if one were still more inquisitive he could further inform himself as to the electrical tension of the atmosphere and other matters of like import. That such knowledge could be gleaned without a visit to the open air was an obvious advantage to those who were clothing themselves to face it, whilst the ability to study the variation of a storm without exposure savoured of no light victory of mind over matter.

The dark-room stands next to the parasitologist's* side of the bench which flanks Sunny Jim's Corner†—an involved sentence. To be more exact, the physicists adjust their instruments and write up books at a bench which projects at right angles to the end wall of the hut; the opposite side of this bench is allotted to Atkinson, who is to write with his back to the dark-room. Atkinson being still absent his corner was unfurnished, and my attention was next claimed by the occupant of the dark-room beyond

* One who investigates parasites: in this case, Atkinson.
† Simpson; for both names *see* list on p. xii.

Atkinson's limit. The art of photography has never been so well housed within the Polar regions and rarely without them. Such a palatial chamber for the development of negatives and prints can only be justified by the quality of the work produced in it, and is only justified in our case by the possession of such an artist as Ponting. He was eager to show me the results of his summer work, and meanwhile my eye took in the neat shelves with their array of cameras, etc., the porcelain sink and automatic water tap, the two acetylene gas burners with their shading screens, and the general obviousness of all conveniences of the photographic art. Here, indeed, was encouragement for the best results, and to the photographer be all praise, for it is mainly his hand which has executed the designs which his brain conceived. In this may be clearly seen the advantage of a traveller's experience. Ponting has had to provide for himself under primitive conditions in a new land; the result is a 'handy man' with every form of tool and in any circumstances. Thus, when building operations were to the fore and mechanical labour scarce, Ponting returned to the shell of his apartment with only the raw material for completing it. In the shortest possible space of time shelves and tanks were erected, doors hung and windows framed, and all in a workmanlike manner commanding the admiration of all beholders. It was well that speed could be commanded for such work, since the fleeting hours of the summer season had been altogether too few to be spared from the immediate service of photography. Ponting's nervous temperament allowed no waste of time—for him fine weather meant no sleep; he decided that lost opportunities should be as rare as circumstances would permit.

This attitude was now manifested in the many yards of cinematograph film remaining on hand and yet greater number recorded as having been sent back in the ship,* in the boxes of negatives lying on the shelves and a well-filled album of prints.

Of the many admirable points in this work, perhaps the most notable are Ponting's eye for a picture and the mastery he has acquired of ice subjects; the composition of most of his pictures is extraordinarily good, he seems to know by instinct the exact value of foreground and middle distance and of the introduction of 'life,' whilst with more technical skill in the manipulation of screens and exposures he emphasises the subtle shadows of the snow and reproduces its wondrously transparent texture. It is good to hear his enthusiasm for results of the past and plans for the future.

Long before I could gaze my fill at the contents of the dark-room I was led to the biologist's cubicle; Nelson and Day had from the first decided to camp together, each having a habit of methodical neatness; both were greatly relieved when the arrangement was approved, and they were freed from the chance of an untidy companion. No attempt had been made to furnish this cubicle before our departure on the autumn journey, but now on my return I found it an example of the best utilisation of space. The prevailing note was neatness; the biologist's microscope stood on a neat bench surrounded by enamel dishes, vessels, and books neatly arranged; behind him, when seated, rose two neat bunks with neat, closely curtained drawers for clothing and neat reflecting sconces for candles; overhead was a neat arrangement for drying socks, with

* When it left for the North on January 25th.

several nets, neatly bestowed. The carpentering to produce this effect had been of quite a high order, and was in very marked contrast with that exhibited for the hasty erections in other cubicles. The pillars and boarding of the bunks had carefully finished edges and were stained to mahogany brown. Nelson's bench is situated very conveniently under the largest of the hut windows, and had also an acetylene lamp, so that both in summer and winter he has all conveniences for his indoor work.

Day appeared to have been unceasingly busy during my absence. Every one paid tribute to his mechanical skill and expressed gratitude for the help he had given in adjusting instruments and generally helping forward the scientific work. He was entirely responsible for the heating, lighting, and ventilating arrangements, and as all these appear satisfactory he deserved much praise. Particulars concerning these arrangements I shall give later; as a first impression it is sufficient to note that the warmth and lighting of the hut seemed as good as could be desired, whilst for our comfort the air seemed fresh and pure. Day had also to report some progress with the motor sledges, but this matter also I leave for future consideration.

My attention was very naturally turned from the heating arrangements to the cooking stove and its custodian, Clissold. I had already heard much of the surpassingly satisfactory meals which his art had produced, and had indeed already a first experience of them. Now I was introduced to the cook's corner with its range and ovens, its pots and pans, its side tables and well-covered shelves. Much was to be gathered therefrom, although a good meal by no means depends only on kitchen conveniences. It was gratifying to learn that the stove had proved itself economical and the patent fuel blocks a most convenient and efficient substitute for coal. Save for the thickness of the furnace cheeks and the size of the oven, Clissold declared himself wholly satisfied. He feared that the oven would prove too small to keep up a constant supply of bread for all hands; nevertheless he introduced me to this oven with an air of pride which I soon found to be fully justified. For connected therewith was a contrivance for which he was entirely responsible, and which in its ingenuity rivalled any of which the hut could boast. The interior of the oven was so arranged that the 'rising' of the bread completed an electric circuit, thereby ringing a bell and switching on a red lamp. Clissold had realised that the continuous ringing of the bell would not be soothing to the nerves of our party, nor the continuous burning of the lamp calculated to prolong its life, and he had therefore added the clock-work mechanism which automatically broke the circuit after a short interval of time; further, this clockwork mechanism could be made to secure the repetition of the same warning signals at intervals of time varied according to the desire of the operator;—thus because, when in bed, he would desire a signal at short periods, but if absent from the hut he would wish to know at a glance what had happened when he returned. Judged by any standard it was a remarkably pretty little device, but when I learnt that it had been made from odds and ends, such as a cog-wheel or spring here and a cell or magnet there, begged from other departments, I began to realise that we had a very exceptional cook. Later, when I found that Clissold was called in to consult on the ailments of Simpson's motor and that he was capable of constructing a dog sledge out of packing cases, I was less surprised, because I knew

A dog sledge at the foot of Castle Berg

An ice grotto (Captain Scott and Wright)

by this time that he had had considerable training in mechanical work before he turned his attention to pots and pans.

My first impressions include matters to which I was naturally eager to give an early half-hour, namely, the housing of our animals. I found herein that praise was as justly due to our Russian boys as to my fellow Englishmen. Anton, with Lashly's help, had completed the furnishing of the stables. Neat stalls occupied the whole length of the 'lean-to,' the sides so boarded that sprawling legs could not be entangled beneath and the front well covered with tin sheet to defeat the 'cribbers.'* I could but sigh again to think of the stalls that must now remain empty, whilst appreciating that there was ample room for the safe harbouring of the ten beasts that remained, be the winter never so cold or the winds so wild.

Later we have been able to give double space to all but two or three of our animals, in which they can lie down if they are so inclined.

The ponies looked fairly fit considering the low diet on which they had been kept; their coats were surprisingly long and woolly in contrast with those of the animals I had left at Hut Point. At this time they were being exercised by Lashly, Anton, Demetri, Hooper, and Clissold, and as a rule were ridden, the sea having only recently frozen. The exercise ground had lain on the boulder-strewn sand of the home beach and extending towards the Skua lake; and across these stretches I soon saw barebacked figures dashing at speed, and not a few amusing incidents in which horse and rider parted with abrupt lack of ceremony. I didn't think this quite the most desirable form of exercise

---

* Or crib-biters: horses given to biting the manger.

for the beasts, but decided to leave matters as they were till our pony manager returned.

Demetri had only five or six dogs left in charge, but these looked fairly fit, all things considered, and it was evident the boy was bent on taking every care of them, for he had not only provided shelters, but had built a small 'lean-to' which would serve as a hospital for any animal whose stomach or coat needed nursing.

Such were in broad outline the impressions I received on my first return to our home station; they were almost wholly pleasant and in happy contrast with the fears that had assailed me on the homeward route. As the days went by I was able to fill in the detail in equally pleasant fashion, to watch the development of fresh arrangements and the improvement of old ones. Finally, in this way I was brought to realise what an extensive and intricate but eminently satisfactory organisation I had made myself responsible for.

# 7

# The Work and the Workers

*Tuesday, May 2.*—To-day have had our first game of football; a harassing southerly wind sprang up, which helped my own side to the extent of three goals.

*Friday, May 5.*—One sees Wilson busy with pencil and colour box, rapidly and steadily adding to his port-folio of charming sketches and at intervals filling the gaps in his zoological work of *Discovery* times; withal ready and willing to give advice and assistance to others at all times; his sound judgment is appreciated and therefore he is a constant referee.

Simpson, master of his craft, untiringly attentive to the working of his numerous self-recording instruments, observing all changes with scientific discernment, doing the work of two observers at least, and yet ever seeking to extend the scope of his observations. So the current meteorological and magnetic readings are taken as never before by Polar expeditions.

Wright, good-hearted, strong, keen, striving to saturate his mind with the ice problems of this wonderful region. He has taken the electrical work in hand with all its modern interest of association with radio-activity.

Evans, with a clear-minded zeal in his own work, does it with all the success of result which comes from the taking of pains. Therefrom we derive a singularly exact preservation of time—an important consideration to all, but especially necessary for the physical work. Therefrom also, and including more labour, we have an accurate survey of our immediate surroundings and are sure we possess the correctly mapped results of all surveying data obtained. He has Gran for assistant.

Taylor's intellect is omnivorous and versatile—his mind is unceasingly active, his grasp wide. Whatever he writes will be of interest—his pen flows well.

Debenham's is clearer. Here we have a well-trained, sturdy worker, with a quiet meaning that carries conviction; he realises the conceptions of thoroughness and conscientiousness.

To Bowers' practical genius is owed much of the smooth working of our station. He has a natural method in line with which all arrangements fall, so that expenditure is easily and exactly adjusted to supply, and I have the inestimable advantage of knowing the length of time which each of our possessions will last us and the assurance that there can be no waste. Active mind and active body were never more happily blended. It is a restless activity, admitting no idle moments and ever budding into new forms.

So we see the balloon ascending under his guidance and anon he is away over the floe tracking the silk thread which held it. Such a task completed, he is away to exercise his pony, and later out again with the dogs, the last typically self-suggested, because for the moment there is no one else to care for these animals. Now in a similar manner he is spreading thermometer screens to get comparative readings with the home station. He is for the open air, seemingly incapable of realising any discomfort from it, and yet his hours within doors are spent with equal profit.

For he is intent on tracking the problems of sledging food and clothing to their innermost bearings and is becoming an authority on past records. This will be no small help to me and one which others never could have given.

Adjacent to the physicists' corner of the hut Atkinson is quietly pursuing the subject of parasites. Already he is in a new world. The laying out of the fish trap was his action and the catches are his field of labour. Constantly he comes to ask if I would like to see some new form, and I am taken to see some protozoa or ascidian* isolated on the slide plate of his microscope. The fishes themselves are comparatively new to science; it is strange that their parasites should have been under investigation so soon.

Atkinson's bench with its array of microscopes, test-tubes, spirit lamps, etc., is next the dark-room in which Ponting spends the greater part of his life.

Cherry-Garrard is another of the open-air, self-effacing, quiet workers; his whole heart is in the life, with profound eagerness to help every one. 'One has caught glimpses of him in tight places; sound all through and pretty hard also.' Indoors he is editing our Polar journal, out of doors he is busy making trial stone huts and blubber stoves, primarily with a view to the winter journey to Cape Crozier, but incidentally these are instructive experiments for any party which may get into difficulty by being cut off from the home station. It is very well to know how best to use the scant resources that Nature provides in these regions. In this connection I have been studying our Arctic library to get details concerning snow-hut building and the implements used for it.

Oates' whole heart is in the ponies. He is really devoted

* Microscopic animals, of a very simple type.

to their care, and I believe will produce them in the best possible form for the sledging season. Opening out the stores, installing a blubber stove, etc., has kept *him* busy, whilst his satellite, Anton, is ever at work in the stables—an excellent little man.

P.O. Evans and Crean are repairing sleeping-bags, covering felt boots, and generally working on sledging kit. In fact, there is no one idle, and no one who has the least prospect of idleness.

*Sunday, May 7.*—Daylight now is very short. Bowers and Cherry-Garrard have set up a thermometer screen containing maximum thermometers and thermographs on the sea floe about $\frac{3}{4}'$ N.W. of the hut. Another smaller one is to go on top of the Ramp. They took the screen out on one of Day's bicycle-wheel carriages and found it ran very easily over the salty ice where the sledges give so much trouble. This vehicle is not easily turned, but may be very useful before there is much snowfall.

Yesterday a balloon was sent up and reached a very good height (probably 2 to 3 miles) before the instrument disengaged; the balloon went almost straight up and the silk fell in festoons over the rocky part of the Cape, affording a very difficult clue to follow; but whilst Bowers was following it, Atkinson observed the instrument fall a few hundred yards out on the Bay—it was recovered and gives the first important record of upper-air temperature.

Atkinson and Crean put out the fish trap in about 3 fathoms of water off the west beach; both yesterday morning and yesterday evening, when the trap was raised it contained over forty fish, whilst this morning and this evening the catches in the same spot have been from twenty to twenty-five. We had fish for breakfast this morning, but an even more satisfactory result of the catches has been revealed by Atkinson's microscope. He has discovered quite a number of new parasites and found work to last quite a long time.

Last night it came to my turn to do night watchman again, so that I shall be glad to have a good sleep to-night.

Yesterday we had a game of football; it is pleasant to mess about, but the light is failing.

Clissold is still producing food novelties; to-night we had galantine of seal—it was *excellent*.

*Monday, May 8—Tuesday, May 9.*—As one of the series of lectures I gave an outline of my plans for next season on Monday evening. Every one was interested, naturally. I could not but hint that in my opinion the problem of reaching the Pole can best be solved by relying on the ponies and man haulage. With this sentiment the whole company appeared to be in sympathy. Every one seems to distrust the dogs when it comes to glacier and summit. I have asked every one to give thought to the problem, to freely discuss it, and bring suggestions to my notice. It's going to be a tough job; that is better realised the more one dives into it.

# 8

# In Winter Quarters: Modern Style

*Sunday, May 21.*—To-night we had a glorious auroral display—quite the most brilliant I have seen. At one time the sky from N.N.W. to S.S.E. as high as the zenith was massed with arches, band, and curtains, always in rapid movement. The waving curtains were especially fascinating—a wave of bright light would start at one end and run along to the other, or a patch of brighter light would spread as if to reinforce the failing light of the curtain.

The auroral light is of a palish green colour, but we now see distinctly a red flush preceding the motion of any bright part.

The green ghostly light seems suddenly to spring to life with rosy blushes. There is infinite suggestion in this phenomenon, and in that lies its charm; the suggestion of life, form, colour, and movement never less than evanescent, mysterious—no reality. It is the language of mystic signs and portents—the inspiration of the gods—wholly spiritual —divine signalling. Remindful of superstition, provocative of imagination. Might not the inhabitants of some other world (Mars) controlling mighty forces thus surround our globe with fiery symbols, a golden writing which we have not the key to decipher?

*Friday, May 26.*—We are living extraordinarily well. At dinner last night we had some excellent thick seal soup, very much like thick hare soup; this was followed by an equally tasty seal steak and kidney pie and a fruit jelly. The smell of frying greeted us on awaking this morning, and at breakfast each of us had two of our nutty little *Notothenia* fish after our bowl of porridge. These little fish have an extraordinarily sweet taste—bread and butter and marmalade finished the meal. At the midday meal we had bread and butter, cheese, and cake, and to-night I smell mutton in the preparation. Under the circumstances it would be difficult to conceive more appetising repasts or a régime which is less likely to produce scorbutic* symptoms. I cannot think we shall get scurvy.

*Monday, May 29.*—Lecture—Japan. To-night Ponting gave us a charming lecture on Japan with wonderful illustrations of his own. He is happiest in his descriptions of the artistic side of the people with which he is in fullest sympathy. So he took us to see the flower pageants: the joyful festivals of the cherry blossom, the wistaria, the iris and chrysanthemum, the sombre colours of the beech blossom and the paths about the lotus gardens, where mankind meditated in solemn mood. We had pictures, too, of Nikko and its beauties, of Temples and great Buddhas. Then in more touristy strain of volcanoes and their craters, waterfalls and river gorges, tiny tree-clad islets, that feature of Japan—baths and their bathers, Ainos, and so on. His descriptions were well given and we all of us thoroughly enjoyed our evening.

*Wednesday, May 31.*—To-night Wilson has given us a very interesting lecture on sketching. He started by explaining his methods of rough sketch and written colour record, and explained its suitability to this climate as

* Of scurvy, caused by vitamin deficiency.

opposed to coloured chalks, etc.—a very practical method for cold fingers and one that becomes more accurate with practice in observation. His theme then became the extreme importance of accuracy, his mode of expression and explanation frankly Ruskinesque.* Don't put in meaningless lines—every line should be from observation. So with contrast of light and shade, fine shading, subtle distinction, everything—impossible without care, patience, and trained attention.

He raised a smile by explaining failures in sketches of others of our party which had been brought to him for criticism. He pointed out how much had been put in from preconceived notion. 'He will draw a berg faithfully as it is now and he studies it, but he leaves sea and sky to be put in afterwards, as he thinks they must be like sea and sky everywhere else, and he is content to try and remember how these *should* be done.' Nature's harmonies cannot be guessed at. He quoted much from Ruskin, leading on a little deeper to 'Composition.'

The lecture was delivered in the author's usual modest strain, but unconsciously it was expressive of himself and his whole-hearted thoroughness. He stands very high in the scale of human beings—how high I scarcely knew till the experience of the past few months.

There is no member of our party so universally esteemed; only to-night I realise how patiently and consistently he has given time and attention to help the efforts of the other sketchers, and so it is all through; he has had a hand in almost every lecture given, and has been consulted in almost every effort which has been made towards the

* Based on the teaching of John Ruskin, the eminent art critic and writer.

solution of the practical or theoretical problems of our Polar world.

The achievement of a great result by patient work is the best possible object-lesson for struggling humanity, for the results of genius, however admirable, can rarely be instructive. The chief of the Scientific Staff sets an example which is more potent than any other factor in maintaining that bond of good fellowship which is the marked and beneficent characteristic of our community.

# 9

# To Midwinter Day

*Tuesday, June 6.*—It is my birthday, a fact I might easily have forgotten, but my kind people did not. At lunch an immense birthday cake made its appearance and we were photographed assembling about it. Clissold had decorated its sugared top with various devices in chocolate and crystallised fruit, flags and photographs of myself.

After my walk I discovered that great preparations were in progress for a special dinner, and when the hour for that meal arrived we sat down to a sumptuous spread with our sledge banners hung about us. Clissold's especially excellent seal soup, roast mutton and red currant jelly, fruit salad, asparagus and chocolate—such was our menu. For drink we had cider cup, a mystery not yet fathomed, some sherry and a liqueur.

After this luxurious meal every one was very festive and amiably argumentative. As I write there is a group in the dark-room discussing political progress with large discussions—another at one corner of the dinner table airing its views on the origin of matter and the probability of its ultimate discovery, and yet another debating military problems. The scraps that reach me from the various groups sometimes piece together in ludicrous fashion. Perhaps these arguments are practically unprofitable, but they give a great deal of pleasure to the participants. It's delightful to hear the ring of triumph in some voice when the owner imagines he has delivered himself of a well-rounded period or a clinching statement concerning the point under discussion. They are boys, all of them, but such excellent good-natured ones; there has been no sign of sharpness or anger, no jarring note, in all these wordy contests; all end with a laugh.

*Monday, June 19.*—A pleasant change to find the air calm and the sky clear—temperature down to −28°. At 1.30 the moon vanished behind the western mountains, after which, in spite of the clear sky, it was very dark on the floe. Went out on ski across the bay, then round about the cape, and so home, facing a keen northerly wind on return.

Atkinson is making a new fish-trap hole; from one cause and another, the breaking of the trap, and the freezing of the hole, no catch has been made for some time. I don't think we shall get good catches during the dark season, but Atkinson's own requirements are small, and the fish, though nice enough, are not such a luxury as to be greatly missed from our 'menu.'

Our daily routine has possessed a settled regularity for a long time. Clissold is up about 7 A.M. to start the breakfast. At 7.30 Hooper starts sweeping the floor and setting the table. Between 8 and 8.30 the men are out and about, fetching ice for melting, etc. Anton is off to feed the ponies, Demetri to see the dogs; Hooper bursts on the slumberers with repeated announcements of the time, usually a quarter of an hour ahead of the clock. There is a stretching of limbs and an interchange of morning greetings, garnished with sleepy humour. Wilson and Bowers meet in a state of nature beside a washing basin filled with snow and proceed to rub glistening limbs with this chilling substance. A little later with less hardihood some others may be seen making the most of a meagre allowance of water. Soon after 8.30 I manage to drag myself from a very comfortable bed and make my toilet with a bare pint of water. By about ten minutes to 9 my clothes are on, my bed is made, and I sit down to my bowl of porridge; most of the others are gathered about the table by this time, but there are a few laggards who run the nine o'clock rule very close. The rule is instituted to prevent delay in the day's work, and it has needed a little pressure to keep one or two up to its observance. By 9.20 breakfast is finished, and before the half-hour has struck the table has been cleared. From 9.30 to 1.30 the men are steadily employed on a programme of preparation for sledging, which seems likely to occupy the greater part of the winter. The repair of sleeping-bags and the alteration of tents have already been done, but there are many other tasks uncompleted or not yet begun, such as the manufacture of provision bags, crampons,* sealskin soles, pony clothes, etc.

Hooper has another good sweep up the hut after breakfast, washes the mess traps,† and generally tidies things. I think it a good thing that in these matters the officers need not wait on themselves; it gives long unbroken days of scientific work and must, therefore, be an economy of brain in the long run.

We meet for our mid-day meal at 1.30 or 1.45, and spend a very cheerful half-hour over it. Afterwards the ponies are exercised, weather permitting; this employs all the men and a few of the officers for an hour or more—the rest of us generally take exercise in some form at the same time. After this the officers go on steadily with their work,

* Iron fittings, to grip the ice.
† The dishes used for the meal.

whilst the men do odd jobs to while away the time. The evening meal, our dinner, comes at 6.30, and is finished within the hour. Afterwards people read, write, or play games, or occasionally finish some piece of work. The gramophone is usually started by some kindly disposed person, and on three nights of the week the lectures to which I have referred are given. They still command full audiences and lively discussions.

At 11 P.M. the acetylene lights are put out, and those who wish to remain up or to read in bed must depend on candle-light. The majority of candles are extinguished by midnight, and the night watchman alone remains awake to keep his vigil by the light of an oil lamp.

Day after day passes in this fashion. It is not a very active life perhaps, but certainly not an idle one. Few of us sleep more than eight hours out of the twenty-four. On Saturday afternoon or Sunday morning some extra bathing takes place; chins are shaved, and perhaps clean garments donned. Such signs, with the regular Service on Sunday, mark the passage of the weeks.

*Thursday, June 22.*—MIDWINTER. The sun reached its maximum depression at about 2.30 P.M. on the 22nd, Greenwich Mean Time: this is 2.30 A.M. on the 23rd according to the local time of the 180th meridian which we are keeping. Dinner to-night is therefore the meal which is nearest the sun's critical change of course, and has been observed with all the festivity customary at Xmas at home.

At tea we broached an enormous Buszard* cake, with much gratitude to its provider, Cherry-Garrard. In preparation for the evening our 'Union Jacks' and sledge flags were hung about the large table, which itself was laid with

* Once a famous confectioner in London.

glass and a plentiful supply of champagne bottles instead of the customary mugs and enamel limejuice jugs. At seven o'clock we sat down to an extravagant bill of fare as compared with our usual simple diet.

Beginning on seal soup, by common consent the best liquid refreshment our cook produces, we went on to roast beef with Yorkshire pudding, fried potatoes and Brussels sprouts. Then followed a flaming plum-pudding and excellent mince-pies, and thereafter a dainty savoury of anchovy and cod's roe. A wondrous attractive meal even in so far as judged by our simple lights, but with its garnishments a positive feast, for withal the table was strewn with dishes of burnt almonds, crystallised fruits, chocolates and such toothsome morsels, whilst the unstinted supply of champagne which accompanied the courses was succeeded by a noble array of liqueur bottles from which choice could be made in the drinking of toasts.

I screwed myself up to a little speech which drew attention to the nature of the celebration as a half-way mark not only in our winter but in the plans of the Expedition as originally published. (I fear there are some who don't realise how rapidly time passes and who have barely begun work which by this time ought to be in full swing.)

We had come through a summer season and half a winter, and had before us half a winter and a second summer. We ought to know how we stood in every respect; we did know how we stood in regard to stores and transport, and I especially thanked the officer in charge of stores and the custodians of the animals. I said that as regards the future, chance must play a part, but that experience showed me that it would have been impossible to have chosen people more fitted to support me in the enterprise to the South than those who were to start in that direction in the spring. I thanked them all for having put their shoulders to the wheel and given me this confidence.

We drank to the Success of the Expedition.

Then every one was called on to speak, starting on my left and working round the table; the result was very characteristic of the various individuals—one seemed to know so well the style of utterance to which each would commit himself.

Needless to say, all were entirely modest and brief; unexpectedly, all had exceedingly kind things to say of me— in fact I was obliged to request the omission of compliments at an early stage. Nevertheless it was gratifying to have a really genuine recognition of my attitude towards the scientific workers of the Expedition, and I felt very warmly towards all these kind, good fellows for expressing it.

If good will and happy fellowship count towards success, very surely shall we deserve to succeed. It was matter for comment, much applauded, that there had not been a single disagreement between any two members of our party from the beginning. By the end of dinner a very cheerful spirit prevailed, and the room was cleared for Ponting and his lantern, whilst the gramophone gave forth its most lively airs.

When the table was upended, its legs removed, and chairs arranged in rows, we had quite a roomy lecture hall. Ponting had cleverly chosen this opportunity to display a series of slides made from his own local negatives. I have never so fully realised his work as on seeing these beautiful pictures; they so easily outclass anything of their kind previously taken in these regions. Our audience cheered vociferously.

After this show the table was restored for snap-dragon, and a brew of milk punch was prepared in which we drank the health of Campbell's Party* and of our good friends in the *Terra Nova*. Then the table was again removed and a set of lancers† formed.

In the midst of the revelry Bowers suddenly appeared, followed by some satellites bearing an enormous Christmas Tree whose branches bore flaming candles, gaudy crackers, and little presents for all. The presents, I learnt, had been prepared with kindly thought by Miss Souper (Mrs. Wilson's sister), and the tree had been made by Bowers of pieces of stick and string, with coloured paper to clothe its branches; the whole erection was remarkably creditable and the distribution of the presents caused much amusement.

Whilst revelry was the order of the day within our hut, the elements without seemed desirous of celebrating the occasion with equal emphasis and greater decorum. The eastern sky was massed with swaying auroral light, the most vivid and beautiful display that I had ever seen—fold on fold the arches and curtains of vibrating luminosity rose and spread across the sky, to fade slowly and yet again spring to glowing life.

The brighter light seemed to flow, now to mass itself in wreathing folds in one quarter, from which lustrous streamers shot upward, and anon to run in waves through the system of some dimmer figure as if to infuse new life within it.

It is impossible to witness such a beautiful phenomenon

---

* The Northern Expedition to King Edward's Land (January 1911—January 1913).

† A round dance, usually by four couples.

without a sense of awe, and yet this sentiment is not inspired by its brilliancy but rather by its delicacy in light and colour, its transparency, and above all by its tremulous evanescence of form. There is no glittering splendour to dazzle the eye, as has been too often described; rather the appeal is to the imagination by the suggestion of something wholly spiritual, something instinct with a fluttering ethereal life, serenely confident yet restlessly mobile.

One wonders why history does not tell us of 'aurora' worshippers, so easily could the phenomenon be considered the manifestation of 'god' or 'demon.' To the little silent group which stood at gaze before such enchantment it seemed profane to return to the mental and physical atmosphere of our house. Finally, when I stepped within, I was glad to find that there had been a general movement bedwards, and in the next half-hour the last of the revellers had succumbed to slumber.

# 10

# The Last Months at Cape Evans

*Wednesday, August 2.*—The Crozier Party returned last night after enduring for five weeks the hardest conditions on record. They looked more weather-worn than anyone I have yet seen. Their faces were scarred and wrinkled, their eyes dull, their hands whitened and creased with the constant exposure to damp and cold, yet the scars of frostbite were very few and this evil had never seriously assailed them. The main part of their afflictions arose, and very obviously arose, from sheer lack of sleep, and to-day after a night's rest our travellers are very different in appearance and mental capacity.

The story of a very wonderful performance must be told by the actors. It is for me now to give but an outline of the journey, and to note more particularly the effects of the strain which they have imposed on themselves and the lessons which their experiences teach for our future guidance.

Wilson is very thin, but this morning very much his keen, wiry self—Bowers is quite himself to-day. Cherry-Garrard is slightly puffy in the face and still looks worn. It is evident that he has suffered most severely—but Wilson

---

* This had been undertaken by Wilson, Bowers and Cherry-Garrard in order to study the Emperor penguin rookery at Cape Crozier (*see* p. 26), observe winter conditions on the Barrier, and experiment with sledging rations.

tells me that his spirit never wavered for a moment. Bowers has come through best, all things considered, and I believe he is the hardest traveller that ever undertook a Polar journey, as well as one of the most undaunted; more by hint than direct statement I gather his value to the party, his untiring energy and the astonishing physique which enables him to continue to work under conditions which are absolutely paralysing to others. Never was such a sturdy, active, undefeatable little man.

So far as one can gather, the story of this journey in brief is much as follows: The party reached the Barrier two days after leaving C. Evans, still pulling their full load of 250 lbs. per man; the snow surface then changed completely and grew worse and worse as they advanced. For one day they struggled on as before, covering 4 miles, but from this onward they were forced to relay,* and found the half load heavier than the whole one had been on the sea ice. Meanwhile the temperature had been falling, and now for more than a week the thermometer fell below −60°. On one night the minimum showed −71°, and on the next −77°, 109° of frost. Although in this truly fearful cold the air was comparatively still, every now and again little puffs of wind came eddying across the snow plain with blighting effect. No civilised being has ever encountered such conditions before with only a tent of thin canvas to rely on for shelter.

It took the best part of a fortnight to cross the coldest region, and then rounding C. Mackay they entered the windswept area. Blizzard followed blizzard, the sky was constantly overcast and they staggered on in a light which was little better than complete darkness; sometimes they

* To go forward with part of the load and return for the rest.

found themselves high on the slopes of Terror* on the left of their track, and sometimes diving into the pressure ridges on the right amidst crevasses and confused ice disturbance. Reaching the foothills near C. Crozier, they ascended 800 feet, then packed† their belongings over a moraine ridge and started to build a hut. It took three days to build the stone walls and complete the roof with the canvas brought for the purpose. Then at last they could attend to the object of the journey.

The scant twilight at midday was so short that they must start in the dark and be prepared for the risk of missing their way in returning without light. On the first day in which they set forth under these conditions it took them two hours to reach the pressure ridges, and to clamber over them roped together occupied nearly the same time; finally they reached a place above the rookery where they could hear the birds squawking, but from which they were quite unable to find a way down. The poor light was failing and they returned to camp. Starting again on the following day they wound their way through frightful ice disturbances under the high basalt cliffs; in places the rock overhung, and at one spot they had to creep through a small channel hollowed in the ice. At last they reached the sea ice, but now the light was so far spent they were obliged to rush everything. Instead of the 2000 or 3000 nesting birds which had been seen here in *Discovery* days, they could now only count about 100; they hastily killed and skinned three to get blubber for their stove, and collecting six eggs, three of which alone survived, they dashed for camp.

* A mountain. *See* map.
† That is, carried them on their backs where they could not take the sledges.

It is possible the birds are deserting this rookery, but it is also possible that this early date found only a small minority of the birds which will be collected at a later one. The eggs, which have not yet been examined, should throw light on this point. Wilson observed yet another proof of the strength of the nursing instinct in these birds. In searching for eggs both he and Bowers picked up rounded pieces of ice which these ridiculous creatures had been cherishing with fond hope.

The light had failed entirely by the time the party were clear of the pressure ridges on their return, and it was only by good luck they regained their camp.

That night a blizzard commenced, increasing in fury from moment to moment. They now found that the place chosen for the hut for shelter was worse than useless. They had far better have built it in the open, for the fierce wind, instead of striking them directly, was deflected on to them in furious whirling gusts. Heavy blocks of snow and rock placed on the roof were whirled away and the canvas ballooned up, tearing and straining at its securings—its disappearance could only be a question of time. They had erected their tent with some valuables inside close to the hut; it had been well spread and more than amply secured with snow and boulders, but one terrific gust tore it up and whirled it away. Inside the hut they waited for the roof to vanish, wondering what they could do if it went, and vainly endeavouring to make it secure. After fourteen hours it went, as they were trying to pin down one corner. The smother of snow was on them and they could only dive for their sleeping-bags with a gasp. Bowers put his head out once and said, 'We're all right,' in as near his ordinary tones as he could compass. The others replied, 'Yes, we're all right,' and all were silent for a night and half a day whilst the wind howled on; the snow entered every chink and crevice of the sleeping-bags, and the occupants shivered and wondered how it would all end.

The wind fell at noon the following day; the forlorn travellers crept from their icy nests, made shift to spread their floorcloth overhead, and lit their primus. They tasted their first food for forty-eight hours and began to plan a means to build a shelter on the homeward route. They decided that they must dig a large pit nightly and cover it as best they could with their floorcloth. But now fortune befriended them; a search to the north revealed the tent lying amongst boulders a quarter of a mile away, and, strange to relate, practically uninjured, a fine testimonial for the material used in its construction. On the following day they started homeward, and immediately another blizzard fell on them, holding them prisoners for two days. By this time the miserable condition of their effects was beyond description. The sleeping-bags were far too stiff to be rolled up, in fact they were so hard frozen that attempts to bend them actually split the skins; the eiderdown bags inside Wilson's and C.-G.'s reindeer covers served but to fitfully stop the gaps made by such rents. All socks, finnesko, and mits had long been coated with ice; placed in breast pockets or inside vests at night they did not even show signs of thawing, much less of drying. It sometimes took C.-G. three-quarters of an hour to get into his sleeping bag, so flat did it freeze and so difficult was it to open. It is scarcely possible to realise the horrible discomforts of the forlorn travellers as they plodded back across the Barrier with the temperature again constantly below $-60°$. In this fashion they reached

Hut Point and on the following night our home quarters.

Wilson is disappointed at seeing so little of the penguins, but to me and to everyone who has remained here the result of this effort is the appeal it makes to our imagination as one of the most gallant stories in Polar History. That men should wander forth in the depth of a Polar night to face the most dismal cold and the fiercest gales in darkness is something new; that they should have persisted in this effort in spite of every adversity for five full weeks is heroic. It makes a tale for our generation which I hope may not be lost in the telling.

Moreover the material results are by no means despicable. We shall know now when that extraordinary bird the Emperor penguin lays its eggs, and under what conditions; but even if our information remains meagre concerning its embryology, our party has shown the nature of the conditions which exist on the Great Barrier in winter. Hitherto we have only imagined their severity; now we have proof, and a positive light is thrown on the local climatology of our Strait.

PREPARATIONS FOR THE SOUTHERN JOURNEY

*Sunday, September 10.*—My whole time has been occupied in making plans for the Southern journey. These are finished at last, I am glad to say; every figure has been checked by Bowers, who has been an enormous help to me. If the motors are successful, we shall have no difficulty in getting to the Glacier, and if they fail, we shall still get there with an ordinary degree of good fortune. To work three units of four men from that point onwards requires no small provision, but with the proper provision it should take a good deal to stop the attainment of our object. I have tried to take every reasonable possibility of misfortune into consideration, and to so organise the parties as to be prepared to meet them. I fear to be too sanguine, yet taking everything into consideration I feel that our chances ought to be good. The animals are in splendid form. Day by day the ponies get fitter as their exercise increases, and stronger, harder food toughens their muscles. They are very different animals from those which we took south last year, and with another month of training I feel there is not one of them but will make light of the loads we shall ask them to draw. But we cannot spare any of the ten, and so there must always be anxiety of the disablement of one or more before their work is done.

It is good to have arrived at a point where we can run over facts and figures again and again without detecting a flaw or foreseeing a difficulty.

I do not count on the motors—that is a strong point in our case—but should they work well, our earlier task of reaching the Glacier will be made quite easy. Apart from such help, I am anxious that these machines should enjoy some measure of success and justify the time, money and thought which have been given to their construction. I am still very confident of the possibility of motor traction, whilst realising that reliance cannot be placed on it in its present untried evolutionary state—it is satisfactory to add that my own view is the most cautious one held in our party. Day is quite convinced he will go a long way, and is prepared to accept much heavier weights than I have given him. Lashly's opinion is perhaps more doubtful, but on the whole hopeful. Clissold is to make the fourth man of the motor party. He has had a great deal of experience with motors, and Day is delighted to have his assistance.

If the Southern journey comes off, nothing, not even priority at the Pole, can prevent the Expedition ranking as one of the most important that ever entered the Polar regions.

*Thursday, September 14.*—Another interregnum. I have been exceedingly busy finishing up the Southern plans, getting instruction in photographing, and preparing for our jaunt to the west. I held forth on the Southern plans yesterday; every one was enthusiastic, and the feeling is general that our arrangements are calculated to make the best of our resources. Although people have given a good deal of thought to various branches of the subject, there was not a suggestion offered for improvement. The scheme seems to have earned full confidence: it remains to play the game out.

'*October, 1911.*—I don't know what to think of Amundsen's* chances. If he gets to the Pole, it must be before we do, as he is bound to travel fast with dogs and pretty certain to start early. On this account I decided at a very early date to act exactly as I should have done had he not existed. Any attempt to race must have wrecked my plan, besides which it doesn't appear the sort of thing one is out for.

'Possibly you will have heard something before this reaches you. Oh! and there are all sorts of possibilities. In any case you can rely on my not doing or saying anything foolish— only I'm afraid you must be prepared for the chance of finding our venture much belittled.

'After all, it is the work that counts, not the applause that follows.

* The Norwegian explorer, who was first at the Pole, a whole month before Scott. *See* Map and p. 128 *et seq*.

'Words must always fail me when I talk of Bill Wilson. I believe he really is the finest character I ever met—the closer one gets to him the more there is to admire. Every quality is so solid and dependable; cannot you imagine how that counts down here? Whatever the matter, one knows Bill will be sound, shrewdly practical, intensely loyal and quite unselfish. Add to this a wider knowledge of persons and things than is at first guessable, a quiet vein of humour and really consummate tact, and you have some idea of his values. I think he is the most popular member of the party, and that is saying much.

'Bowers is all and more than I ever expected of him. He is a positive treasure, absolutely trustworthy and prodigiously energetic. He is about the hardest man amongst us, and that is saying a good deal—nothing seems to hurt his tough little body and certainly no hardship daunts his spirit. I shall have a hundred little tales to tell you of his indefatigable zeal, his unselfishness, and his inextinguishable good humour. He surprises always, for his intelligence is of quite a high order and his memory for details most exceptional. You can imagine him, as he is, an indispensable assistant to me in every detail concerning the management and organisation of our sledging work and a delightful companion on the march.

'One of the greatest successes is Wright. He is very thorough and absolutely ready for anything. Like Bowers he has taken to sledging like a duck to water, and although he hasn't had such severe testing, I believe he would stand it pretty nearly as well. Nothing ever seems to worry him, and I can't imagine he ever complained of anything in his life.

'I don't think I will give such long descriptions of the

others, though most of them deserve equally high praise. Taken all round they are a perfectly excellent lot.

'The Soldier is very popular with all—a delightfully humorous cheery old pessimist—striving with the ponies night and day and bringing woeful accounts of their small ailments into the hut.

'The men are equally fine. Edgar Evans has proved a useful member of our party; he looks after our sledges and sledge equipment with a care of management and a fertility of resource which is truly astonishing—on "trek" he is just as sound and hard as ever and has an inexhaustible store of anecdote.

'Crean is perfectly happy, ready to do anything and go anywhere, the harder the work, the better. Evans and Crean are great friends. Lashly is his old self in every respect, hard-working to the limit, quiet, abstemious, and determined. You see altogether I have a good set of people with me, and it will go hard if we don't achieve something.

'The study of individual character is a pleasant pastime in such a mixed community of thoroughly nice people, and the study of relationships and influences is fascinating— men of the most diverse upbringing and experience are really pals with one another, and the subjects which would be delicate ground of discussion between acquaintances are just those which are most freely used for jest. For instance, the Soldier is never tired of jeering at Australia, its people and institutions, and the Australians retaliate by attacking the hide-bound prejudices of the British Army. I have never seen a temper lost in these discussions. So as I sit here I am very satisfied with these things. I think that it would have been difficult to better the organisation of the party—every man has his work and is especially adapted for it; there is no gap and no overlap—it is all that I desired, and the same might be said of the men selected to do the work.'

*Friday, October 6.*—To-day Wilson, Oates, Cherry-Garrard and Crean have gone to Hut Point with their ponies, Oates getting off with Christopher after some difficulty. At 5 o'clock the Hut Point telephone bell suddenly rang (the line was laid by Meares some time ago, but hitherto there has been no communication). In a minute or two we heard a voice, and behold! communication was established. I had quite a talk with Meares and afterwards with Oates. Not a very wonderful fact, perhaps, but it seems wonderful in this primitive land to be talking to one's fellow beings 15 miles away. Oates told me that the ponies had arrived in fine order, Christopher a little done, but carrying the heaviest load. . . .

The photography craze is in full swing. Ponting's mastery is ever more impressive, and his pupils improve day by day; nearly all of us have produced good negatives.

*Saturday, October 7.*—As though to contradict the suggestion of incompetence, friend 'Jehu' pulled with a will this morning—he covered $3\frac{1}{2}$ miles without a stop, the surface being much worse than it was two days ago. He was not at all distressed when he stopped. If he goes on like this he comes into practical politics again, and I am arranging to give 10-feet sledges to him and Chinaman instead of 12-feet. Probably they will not do much, but if they go on as at present, we shall get something out of them.

Long and cheerful conversations with Hut Point and of course an opportunity for the exchange of witticisms. . . .

*Friday, October 13.*—The ponies have been behaving well, with exceptions. Victor is now quite easy to manage, thanks to Bowers' patience. Chinaman goes along very steadily and is not going to be the crock we expected. He has a slow pace which may be troublesome, but when the weather is fine that won't matter if he can get along steadily.

The most troublesome animal is Christopher. He is only a source of amusement as long as there is no accident, but I am always a little anxious that he will kick or bite someone. The curious thing is that he is quiet enough to handle for walking or riding exercise or in the stable, but as soon as a sledge comes into the programme he is seized with a very demon of viciousness, and bites and kicks with every intent to do injury.

THE START OF THE MOTOR SLEDGES

*Tuesday, October 24.*—Two fine days for a wonder. Yesterday the motors seemed ready to start and we all went out on the floe to give them a 'send off.' But the inevitable little defects cropped up, and the machines only got as far as the Cape. A change made by Day in the working of the petrol engines had caused their internal mechanism to go wrong, so he and Lashly spent the afternoon making good the defects, which they accomplished in a satisfactory manner.

This morning the engines were set going again, and shortly after 10 A.M. a fresh start was made. At first there were a good many stops, but on the whole the engines seemed to be improving all the time. They are not by any means working up to full power yet, and so the pace is very slow. The weights seem to me a good deal heavier than we bargained for. Day sets his motor going, climbs off the car, and walks alongside with an occasional finger on the throttle. Lashly hasn't yet quite got hold of the nice adjustments of his control levers, but I hope will have done so after a day's practice.

The only alarming incident was the slipping of the chains when Day tried to start on some ice very thinly covered with snow. The starting effort on such heavily laden sledges is very heavy, but I thought the grip of the pattens and studs* would have been good enough on any surface. Looking at the place afterwards I found that the studs had grooved the ice.

Now as I write at 12.30 the machines are about a mile out in the South Bay; both can be seen still under way, progressing steadily if slowly.

I find myself immensely eager that these tractors should succeed, even though they may not be of great help to our southern advance. A small measure of success will be enough to show their possibilities, their ability to revolutionise Polar transport. Seeing the machines at work to-day, and remembering that every defect so far shown is purely mechanical, it is impossible not to be convinced of their value. But the trifling mechanical defects and lack of experience show the risk of dispensing with trials. A season of experiment with a small workshop at hand may be all that stands between success and failure.

At any rate before we start we shall certainly know if the worst has happened, or if some measure of success attends this unique effort.

*Thursday, October 26.*—This morning Simpson has just rung up. He says the motors are in difficulties with the surface. The trouble is just that which I noted as alarming

* Blocks and metal buttons for gripping the ground. The sledges were driven by caterpillar chains, like tanks.

on Monday—the chains slip on the very light snow covering of hard ice. The engines are working well, and all goes well when the machines get on to snow.

I have organised a party of eight men, including myself, and we are just off to see what can be done to help.

# 11

# Southern Journey: the Barrier Stage

*Friday, November 3.*—Camp 1. A keen wind with some drift at Hut Point, but we sailed away in detachments. Atkinson's party, Jehu, Chinaman, and Jimmy Pigg led off at eight. Just before ten Wilson, Cherry-Garrard, and I left. Our ponies marched steadily and well together over the sea ice. The wind dropped a good deal, but the temperature with it, so that the little remaining was very cutting. We found Atkinson at Safety Camp. He had lunched and was just ready to march out again; he reports Chinaman and Jehu tired. Ponting arrived soon after we had camped with Demetri and a small dog team. The cinematograph was up in time to catch the flying rearguard which came along in fine form, Snatcher leading and being stopped every now and again—a wonderful little beast. Christopher had given the usual trouble when harnessed, but was evidently subdued by the Barrier Surface. However, it was not thought advisable to halt him, and so the party fled through in the wake of the advance guard.

After lunch we packed up and marched on steadily as before. I don't like these midnight lunches, but for man the march that follows is pleasant when, as to-day, the wind falls and the sun steadily increases its heat. The two parties in front of us camped 5 miles beyond Safety Camp, and we reached their camp some half or three-quarters of an hour later. All the ponies are tethered in good order, but most of them are tired—Chinaman and Jehu *very tired*. Nearly all are inclined to be off feed, but this is very temporary, I think. We have built walls, but there is no wind and the sun gets warmer every minute.

*Mirage*.—Very marked waving effect to east. Small objects greatly exaggerated and showing as dark vertical lines.

1 P.M.—Feeding time. Woke the party, and Oates served out the rations—all ponies feeding well. It is a sweltering day, the air breathless, the glare intense—one loses sight of the fact that the temperature is low ($+22°$)—one's mind seeks comparison in hot sunlit streets and scorching pavements, yet six hours ago my thumb was frostbitten. All the inconveniences of frozen footwear and damp clothes and sleeping-bags have vanished entirely.

*Saturday, November 4*.—Camp 2. Led march—started in what I think will now become the settled order. Atkinson went at 8, ours at 10, Bowers, Oates and Co. at 11.15. Just after starting picked up cheerful note and saw cheerful notices saying all well with motors, both going excellently. Day wrote 'Hope to meet in 80° 30′ (Lat.).' Poor chap, within 2 miles he must have had to sing a different tale. It appears they had a bad grind on the morning of the 29th. I suppose the surface was bad and everything seemed to be going wrong. They 'dumped' a good deal of petrol and lubricant. Worse was to follow. Some 4 miles out we met a tin pathetically inscribed, 'Big end Day's motor No. 2 cylinder broken.' Half a mile beyond, as I expected, we found the motor, its tracking sledges and all. Notes from E. Evans and Day told the tale. The only spare [cylinder] had been used for Lashly's machine, and it would have taken a long time to strip Day's engine so that it could run on three cylinders. They had decided to abandon it and push on with the other alone. They had taken the six bags of forage and some odds and ends, besides their petrol and lubricant. So the dream of great help from the machines is at an end! The track of the remaining motor goes steadily forward, but now, of course, I shall expect to see it every hour of the march.

The ponies did pretty well—a cruel soft surface most of the time, but light loads, of course. Jehu is better than I expected to find him, Chinaman not so well. They are bad crocks both of them.

It was pretty cold during the night, −7° when we camped, with a crisp breeze blowing. The ponies don't like it, but now, as I write, the sun is shining through a white haze, the wind has dropped, and the picketing line is comfortable for the poor beasts.

*Tuesday, November 7.*—Camp 4. A blizzard has continued throughout last night and up to this time of writing, late in the afternoon. Starting mildly, with broken clouds, little snow, and gleams of sunshine, it grew in intensity until this forenoon, when there was heavy snowfall and the sky overspread with low nimbus cloud. In the early afternoon the snow and wind ceased, and the wind is dropping now, but the sky looks very lowering and unsettled.

Last night the sky was so broken that I made certain the end of the blow had come. Towards morning the sky overhead and far to the north was quite clear. More cloud obscured the sun to the south and low heavy banks hung over Ross Island. All seemed hopeful, except that I noted with misgiving that the mantle on the Bluff was beginning to form. Two hours later the whole sky was overcast and the blizzard had fully developed.

This Tuesday evening it remains overcast, but one cannot see that the clouds are travelling fast. The Bluff mantle is a wide low bank of level cloud not particularly windy in appearance; the wind is falling, but the sky still looks lowering to the south, and there is a general appearance of unrest. The temperature has been + 10° all day.

The ponies, which had been so comparatively comfortable in the earlier stages, were distressed as usual when the snow began to fall.

We have done everything possible to shelter and protect them, but there seems no way of keeping them comfortable when the snow is thick and driving fast. We men are snug and comfortable enough, but it is very evil to lie here and know that the weather is steadily sapping the strength of the beasts on which so much depends. It requires much philosophy to be cheerful on such occasions.

In the midst of the drift this forenoon the dog party came up and camped about a quarter of a mile to leeward. Meares has played too much for safety in catching us so soon, but it is satisfactory to find the dogs will pull the loads and can be driven to face such a wind as we have had. It shows that they ought to be able to help us a good deal.

The tents and sledges are badly drifted up, and the drifts behind the pony walls have been dug out several times. I shall be glad indeed to be on the march again, and oh! for a little sun. The ponies are all quite warm when covered by their rugs. Some of the fine drift snow finds its way under the rugs, and especially under the broad belly straps; this melts and makes the coat wet if allowed to remain. It is not easy to understand at first why the blizzard should have such a withering effect on the poor beasts. I think it is mainly due to the exceeding fineness of the snow particles, which, like finely divided powder, penetrate the hair of the coat and lodge in the inner warmths. Here it melts and, as water, carries off the animal heat. Also, no doubt, it harasses the animals by the bombardment of the fine flying particles on tender places such as nostrils, eyes, and to lesser extent ears. In this way it continually bothers them, preventing rest. Of all things the most important for horses is that conditions should be placid whilst they stand tethered.

*Thursday, November 9.*—Camp 6. Sticking to programme, we are going a little over the 10 miles (geo.) nightly. Atkinson started his party at 11 and went on for 7 miles to escape a cold little night breeze which quickly dropped. He was some time at his lunch camp, so that starting to join the rear-guard we came in together the last 2 miles. The experience showed that the slow advance guard ponies are forced out of their pace by joining with the others, whilst the fast rearguard is reduced in speed. Obviously it is not an advantage to be together, yet all the ponies are doing well. An amusing incident happened when Wright left his pony to examine his sledgemeter. Chinaman evidently didn't like being left behind and set off at a canter to rejoin the main body. Wright's long legs barely carried him fast enough to stop this playful stampede, but the ridiculous sight was due to the fact that old Jehu caught the infection and set off at a sprawling canter in Chinaman's wake. As this is the pony we thought scarcely capable of a single march at start, one is agreeably surprised to find him still displaying such commendable spirit. Christopher is troublesome as ever at the start; I fear that signs of tameness will only indicate absence of strength. The dogs followed us so easily over the 10 miles that

Meares thought of going on again, but finally decided that the present easy work is best.

Things look hopeful. The weather is beautiful—temp. +12°, with a bright sun. Some stratus cloud about Discovery and over White Island. The sastrugi* about here are very various in direction and the surface a good deal ploughed up, showing that the Bluff influences the wind direction even out as far as this camp. The surface is hard; I take it about as good as we shall get.

There is an annoying little southerly wind blowing now, and this serves to show the beauty of our snow walls. The ponies are standing under their lee in the bright sun as comfortable as can possibly be.

*Sunday, November 12.*—Camp 9. Our marches are uniformly horrid just at present. The surface remains wretched, not quite so heavy as yesterday, perhaps, but very near it at times. Five miles out the advance party came straight and true on our last year's Bluff depôt marked with a flagstaff. Here following I found a note from E. Evans, cheerful in tone, dated 7 A.M. 7th inst. He is, therefore, the best part of five days ahead of us, which is good. Atkinson camped a mile beyond this cairn and had a very gloomy account of Chinaman. Said he couldn't last more than a mile or two. The weather was horrid, overcast, gloomy, snowy. One's spirits became very low. However, the crocks set off again, the rear-guard came up, passed us in camp, and then on the march about 3 miles on, so that they camped about the same time. The Soldier thinks Chinaman will last for a good many days yet, which is an extraordinary confession of hope for him. The rest of the animals are as well as can be expected—Jehu rather better.

* Snow surfaces, made irregular by the wind.

These weather appearances change every minute. When we camped there was a chill northerly breeze, a black sky, and light falling snow. Now the sky is clearing and the sun shining an hour later. The temperature remains about + 10° in the daytime.

*Wednesday, November 15.*—Camp 12. Found our One Ton Camp without any difficulty [130 geographical miles from Cape Evans]. About 7 or 8 miles. After 5½ miles to lunch camp, Chinaman was pretty tired, but went on again in good form after the rest. All the other ponies made nothing of the march, which, however, was over a distinctly better surface. After a discussion we have decided to give the animals a day's rest here, and then to push forward at the rate of 13 geographical miles a day. Oates thinks the ponies will get through, but that they have lost condition quicker than he expected. Considering his usually pessimistic attitude this must be thought a hopeful view. Personally I am much more hopeful. I think that a good many of the beasts are actually in better form than when they started, and that there is no need to be alarmed about the remainder, always excepting the weak ones, which we have always regarded with doubt. Well, we must wait and see how things go.

*Saturday, November 18.*—Camp 14. The ponies are not pulling well. The surface is, if anything, a little worse than yesterday, but I should think about the sort of thing we shall have to expect henceforward. I had a panic that we were carrying too much food and this morning we have discussed the matter and decided we can leave a sack. We have done the usual 13 miles (geo.) with a few hundred yards to make the 15 statute. The temperature was − 21° when we camped last night, now it is − 3°. The crocks are going on very wonderfully. Oates gives Chinaman at least three days, and Wright says he may go for a week. This is slightly inspiriting, but how much better would it have been to have had ten really reliable beasts! It's touch and go whether we scrape up to the Glacier; meanwhile we get along somehow. At any rate the bright sunshine makes everything *look* more hopeful.

*Sunday, November 19.*—Camp 15. We have struck a real bad surface, sledges pulling well over it, but ponies sinking very deep. The result is to about finish Jehu. He was terribly done on getting in tonight. He may go another march, but not more, I think. Considering the surface the other ponies did well. The ponies occasionally sink halfway to the hock, little Michael once or twice almost to the hock itself. Luckily the weather now is glorious for resting the animals, which are very placid and quiet in the brilliant sun.

*Wednesday, November 22.*—Camp 18. Everything much the same. The ponies thinner but not much weaker. The crocks still going along. Jehu is now called 'The Barrier Wonder' and Chinaman 'The Thunderbolt.' Two days more and they will be well past the spot at which Shackleton killed his first animal. Nobby keeps his pre-eminence of condition and has now the heaviest load by some 50 lbs.; most of the others are under 500 lbs. load, and I hope will be eased further yet. The dogs are in good form still, and came up well with their loads this morning (night temp. −1·4°). It looks as though we ought to get through to the Glacier without great difficulty. The weather is glorious and the ponies can make the most of their rest during the warmest hours, but they certainly lose in one way by marching at night. The surface is much easier for the sledges when the sun is warm, and for about three hours before and after midnight the friction noticeably increases. It is just a question whether this extra weight on the loads is compensated by the resting temperature. We are quite steady on the march now, and though not fast yet get through with few stops. The animals seem to be getting accustomed to the steady, heavy plod and take the deep places less fussily. There is rather an increased condition of false crust—that is, a crust which appears firm till the whole weight of the animal is put upon it, when it suddenly gives some three or four inches. This is very trying for the poor beasts. There are also more patches in which the men sink, so that walking is getting more troublesome, but, speaking broadly, the crusts are not comparatively bad and the surface is rather better than it was. If the hot sun continues this should still further improve. One cannot see any reason why the crust should change in the next 100 miles. (Temp. +2°.)

*Tuesday, November 28.*—Camp 24. The most dismal start imaginable. Thick as a hedge, snow falling and drifting with keen southerly wind. The men pulled out at 3.15 with Chinaman and James Pigg. We followed at 4.20, just catching the party at the lunch camp at 8.30. Things got better half way; the sky showed signs of clearing and the steering improved. Now, at lunch, it is getting thick again. When will the wretched blizzard be over? The walking is better for ponies, worse for men; there is nearly everywhere a hard crust some 3 to 6 inches down. Towards the end of the march we crossed a succession of high hard south-easterly sastrugi, widely dispersed. I don't know what to make of these.

Second march almost as horrid as the first. Wind blowing strong from the south, shifting to S.E. as the snowstorms fell on us, when we could see little or nothing, and the driving snow hit us stingingly in the face. The general impression of all this dirty weather is that it spreads in from the S.E. We started at 4 A.M., and I think I shall stick to that custom for the present. These last few marches have been fought for, but completed without hitch, and, though we camped in a snowstorm, there is a more promising look in the sky, and if only for a time the wind has dropped and the sun shines brightly, dispelling some of the gloomy results of the distressing marching.

Chinaman, 'The Thunderbolt,' has been shot to-night. Plucky little chap, he has stuck it out well and leaves the stage but a few days before his fellows. We have only four bags of forage (each one 130 lbs.) left, but these should give seven marches with all the remaining animals, and we are less than 90 miles from the Glacier. Bowers tells me that the barometer was phenomenally low during this blizzard and the last. This has certainly been the most unexpected and trying summer blizzard yet experienced in this region. I only trust it is over. There is not much to choose between the remaining ponies. Nobby and Bones are the strongest, Victor and Christopher the weakest, but all should get through. The land doesn't show up yet.

*Sunday, December 3.*—Camp 29. Our luck in weather is preposterous. I roused the hands at 2.30 A.M., intending to get away at 5. It was thick and snowy, yet we could have got on; but at breakfast the wind increased, and by 4.30 it was blowing a full gale from the south. The pony wall blew down, huge drifts collected, and the sledges were quickly buried. It was the strongest wind I have known here in summer. At 11 it began to take off. At 12.30 we got up and had lunch and got ready to start. The land appeared, the clouds broke, and by 1.30 we were in bright sunshine. We were off at 2 P.M., the land showing all round, and, but for some cloud to the S.E., everything promising. At 2.15 I saw the south-easterly cloud spreading up; it blotted out the land 30 miles away at 2.30 and was on us before 3. The sun went out, snow fell thickly, and marching conditions became horrible. The wind increased from the S.E., changed to S.W., where it hung for a time, and suddenly shifted to W.N.W. and then N.N.W., from which direction it is now blowing with falling and drifting snow. The changes of conditions are inconceivably rapid, perfectly bewildering. In spite of all these difficulties we have managed to get 11½ miles south and to this camp at 7 P.M. —the conditions of marching simply horrible.

The man-haulers led out 6 miles (geo.) and then camped. I think they had had enough of leading. We passed them, Bowers and I ahead on ski. We steered with compass, the drifting snow across our ski, and occasional glimpse of south-easterly sastrugi under them, till the sun showed dimly for the last hour or so. The whole weather conditions seem thoroughly disturbed, and if they continue so when we are on the Glacier, we shall be very awkwardly placed. It is really time the luck turned in our favour—we have had all too little of it. Every mile seems to have been hardly won under such conditions. The ponies did splendidly and the forage is lasting a little better than expected. Victor was found to have quite a lot of fat on him and the others are pretty certain to have more, so that we should have no difficulty whatever as regards transport if only the weather was kind.

*Tuesday, December 5.*—Camp 30. Noon. We awoke this morning to a raging, howling blizzard. The gales we have had hitherto have lacked the very fine powdery snow—that especial feature of the blizzard. To-day we have it fully developed. After a minute or two in the open one is covered from head to foot. The temperature is high, so that what falls or drives against one sticks. The ponies—heads, tails, legs, and all parts not protected by their rugs—are covered with ice; the animals are standing deep in snow, the sledges are almost covered, and huge drifts above the tents. We have had breakfast, rebuilt the walls, and are now again in our bags. One cannot see the next tent, let alone the land. What on earth does such weather mean at this time of year? It is more than our share of ill-fortune, I think, but the luck may yet turn. I doubt if any party could travel in such weather even with the wind, certainly no one could travel against it.

Is there some widespread atmospheric disturbance which will be felt everywhere in this region as a bad season, or are we merely the victims of exceptional local conditions? If the latter, there is food for thought in picturing our small party struggling against adversity in one place whilst others go smilingly forward in the sunshine. How great may be the element of luck! No foresight—no procedure—could have prepared us for this state of affairs. Had we been ten times as experienced or certain of our aim we should not have expected such rebuffs.

11 P.M.—It has blown hard all day with quite the greatest snowfall I remember. The drifts about the tents are simply huge. The temperature was $+27°$ this forenoon and rose to $+31°$ in the afternoon, at which time the snow melted as it fell on anything but the snow, and, as a consequence, there are pools of water on everything, the tents are wet through, also the wind clothes, night boots,

etc.; water drips from the tent poles and door, lies on the floorcloth, soaks the sleeping-bags, and makes everything pretty wretched. If a cold snap follows before we have had time to dry our things, we shall be mighty uncomfortable. Yet after all it would be humorous enough if it were not for the seriousness of delay—we can't afford that, and it's real hard luck that it should come at such a time. The wind shows signs of easing down, but the temperature does not fall and the snow is as wet as ever—not promising signs of abatement.

*Thursday, December 7.*—Camp 30. The storm continues and the situation is now serious. One small feed remains for the ponies after to-day, so that we must either march to-morrow or sacrifice the animals. That is not the worst; with the help of the dogs we could get on, without doubt. The serious part is that we have this morning started our summit rations—that is to say, the food calculated from the Glacier depôt has been begun. The first supporting party can only go on a fortnight from this date and so forth. The storm shows no sign of abatement and its character is as unpleasant as ever. The promise of last night died away about 3 A.M., when the temperature and wind rose again, and things reverted to the old conditions. I can find no sign of an end, and all of us agree that it is utterly impossible to move. Resignation to misfortune is the only attitude, but not an easy one to adopt. It seems undeserved where plans were well laid and so nearly crowned with a first success. I cannot see that any plan would be altered if it were to do again, the margin for bad weather was ample according to all experience, and this stormy December—our finest month—is a thing that the most cautious organiser might not have been prepared to encounter. It is very evil to lie here in a wet sleeping-bag and think of the pity of it, whilst with no break in the overcast sky things go steadily from bad to worse (T. + 32°). Meares has a bad attack of snow blindness in one eye. I hope this rest will help him, but he says it has been painful for a long time. There cannot be good cheer in the camp in such weather, but it is ready to break out again. In the brief spell of hope last night one heard laughter.

Midnight. Little or no improvement. The barometer is rising—perhaps there is hope in that. Surely few situations could be more exasperating than this of forced inactivity when every day and indeed every hour counts. To be here watching the mottled wet green walls of our tent, the glistening wet bamboos, the bedraggled sopping socks and loose articles dangling in the middle, the saddened countenances of my companions—to hear the everlasting patter of the falling snow and the ceaseless rattle of the fluttering canvas—to feel the wet clinging dampness of clothes and everything touched, and to know that without there is but a blank wall of white on every side—these are the physical surroundings. Add the stress of sighted failure of our whole plan, and any one must find the circumstances unenviable. But yet, after all, one can go on striving, endeavouring to find a stimulation in the difficulties that arise.

*Friday, December 8.*—Camp 30. Hoped against hope for better conditions, to wake to the mournfullest snow and wind as usual. We had breakfast at 10, and at noon the wind dropped. We set about digging out the sledges, no light task. We then shifted our tent sites. All tents had been reduced to the smallest volume by the gradual pressure of snow. The old sites are deep pits with hollowed icy wet centres. The re-setting of the tent has at least given us comfort, especially since the wind has dropped. About 4 the sky showed signs of breaking, the sun and a few patches of land could be dimly discerned. The wind shifted in light airs and a little hope revived. Alas! as I write the sun has disappeared and snow is again falling. Our case is growing desperate. Evans and his man-haulers tried to pull a load this afternoon. They managed to move a sledge with four people on it, pulling in ski. Pulling on foot they sank to the knees. The snow all about us is terribly deep. We tried Nobby and he plunged to his belly in it. Wilson thinks the ponies finished, but Oates thinks they will get another march in spite of the surface, *if it comes to-morrow*. If it should not, we must kill the ponies to-morrow and get on as best we can with the men on ski and the dogs. But one wonders what the dogs can do on such a surface. I much fear they also will prove inadequate. Oh! for fine weather, if only to the Glacier. The temperature remains + 33°, and everything is disgustingly wet.

11 P.M.—The wind has gone to the north, the sky is really breaking at last, the sun showing less sparingly, and the land appearing out of the haze. The temperature has fallen to + 26°, and the water nuisance is already abating. With so fair a promise of improvement it would be too cruel to have to face bad weather to-morrow. There is good cheer in the camp to-night in the prospect of action. The poor ponies look wistfully for the food of which so very little remains, yet they are not hungry, as recent savings have resulted from food left in their nosebags. They look wonderfully fit, all things considered. Everything looks more hopeful to-night, but nothing can recall four lost days.

Stareek, Doctor Wilson's dog team leader

Weddell seal and her calf

Scott's last birthday party. *Left to right*—Atkinson, Meares, Cherry-Garrard, Oates (standing), Taylor, Nelson, Evans, Scott, Wilson, Simpson, Bowers, Gran (standing), Wright, Debenham, Day

*Saturday, December 9.*—Camp 31. I turned out two or three times in the night to find the weather slowly improving; at 5.30 we all got up, and at 8 got away with the ponies—a most painful day. The tremendous snowfall of the late storm had made the surface intolerably soft, and after the first hour there was no glide. We pressed on the poor half-rationed animals, but could get none to lead for more than a few minutes; following, the animals would do fairly well. It looked as if we could never make headway; the man-haulers were pressed into the service to aid matters. Bowers and Cherry-Garrard went ahead with one 10-foot sledge—thus most painfully we made about a mile. The situation was saved by P.O. Evans, who put the last pair of snow-shoes on Snatcher. From this he went on without much pressing, the other ponies followed, and one by one were worn out in the second place. We went on all day without lunch. Three or four miles (T.+23°) found us engulfed in pressures,* but free from difficulty except the awful softness of the snow. By 8 P.M. we had reached within a mile or so of the slope ascending to the gap which Shackleton called the Gateway. I had hoped to be through the Gateway with the ponies still in hand at a very much earlier date and, but for the devastating storm, we should have been. It has been a most serious blow to us, but things are not yet desperate, if only the storm has not hopelessly spoilt the surface. The man-haulers are not up yet, in spite of their light load. I think they have stopped for tea, or something, but under ordinary conditions they would have passed us with ease.

At 8 P.M. the ponies were quite done, one and all. They came on painfully slowly a few hundred yards at a time.

* Heavy, tumbled-up ice, difficult to cross.

9

By this time I was hauling ahead, a ridiculously light load, and yet finding the pulling heavy enough. We camped, and the ponies have been shot.* Poor beasts! they have done wonderfully well considering the terrible circumstances under which they worked, but yet it is hard to have to kill them so early. The dogs are going well in spite of the surface, but here again one cannot get the help one would wish. (T. + 19°.) I cannot load the animals heavily on such snow. The scenery is most impressive; three huge pillars of granite form the right buttress of the Gateway, and a sharp spur of Mount Hope the left. The land is much more snow-covered than when we saw it before the storm. In spite of some doubt in our outlook, every one is very cheerful to-night and jokes are flying freely around.

\* Camp 31 received the name of Shambles Camp.

# 12

# On the Beardmore Glacier

*Sunday, December 10.*—Camp 32. I was very anxious about getting our loads forward over such an appalling surface, and that we had done so is mainly due to the ski. I roused every one at 8, but it was noon before all the readjustments of load had been made and we were ready to start. The dogs carried 600 lbs. of our weight besides the depôt (200 lbs.). It was greatly to my surprise when we—my own party—with a 'one, two, three together' started our sledge, and we found it running fairly easily behind us. We did the first mile at a rate of about 2 miles an hour, having previously very carefully scraped and dried our runners. The day was gloriously fine and we were soon perspiring. After the first mile we began to rise, and for some way on a steep slope we held to our ski and kept going. Then the slope got steeper and the surface much worse, and we had to take off our ski. The pulling after this was extraordinarily fatiguing. We sank above our finnesko everywhere, and in places nearly to our knees. The runners of the sledges got coated with a thin film of ice from which we could not free them, and the sledges themselves sank to the crossbars in soft spots. All the time they were literally ploughing the snow. We reached the top of the slope at 5, and started on after tea on the down grade. On this we had to pull almost as hard as on the upward slope, but could just manage to get along on ski. We camped at 9.15, when a heavy wind coming down the glacier suddenly fell on us; but I had decided to camp before, as Evans' party could not keep up, and Wilson told me some very alarming news concerning it. It appears that Atkinson says that Wright is getting played out and Lashly is not so fit as he was owing to the heavy pulling since the blizzard. I have not felt satisfied about this party. The finish of the march to-day showed clearly that something was wrong. They fell a long way behind, had to take off ski, and took nearly half an hour to come up a few hundred yards. True, the surface was awful and growing worse every moment. It is a very serious business if the men are going to break down. As for myself, I never felt fitter and my party can easily hold its own. P.O. Evans is a tower of strength, but Oates and Wilson are doing splendidly also.

Here where we are camped the snow is worse than I have ever seen it, but we are in a hollow. Every step here one sinks to the knees and the uneven surface is obviously insufficient to support the sledges. Perhaps this wind is a blessing in disguise; already it seems to be hardening the snow. All this soft snow is an aftermath of our prolonged storm. Hereabouts Shackleton found hard blue ice. It seems an extraordinary difference in fortune, and at every step S.'s luck becomes more evident. I take the dogs on for half a day to-morrow, then send them home. We have 200 lbs. to add to each sledge load and could easily do it on a reasonable surface, but it looks very much as though we shall be forced to relay if present conditions hold.

'*Beardmore Glacier*.—Just a tiny note to be taken back by the dogs. Things are not so rosy as they might be, but we keep our spirits up and say the luck must turn. This is only to tell you that I find I can keep up with the rest as well as of old.'*

*Wednesday, December 13.*—Camp 35. A most dismal day. We started at 8—the pulling terribly bad, the glide good; a new crust in patches, not sufficient to support the ski. Therefore, as the pullers got on the hard patches they slipped back. The sledges plunged into the soft places and stopped dead. Evans' party got away first; we followed, and for some time helped them forward at their stops, but this proved altogether too much for us, so I forged ahead and camped at 1 P.M., as the others were far astern. During lunch I decided to try the 10-feet runners under the cross-bars and we spent three hours in securing them. There was no delay on account of the slow progress of the other parties. Evans passed us, and for some time went forward fairly well up a decided slope. The sun was shining on the surface by this time, and the temperature high. Bowers started after Evans, and it was easy to see the really terrible state of affairs with them. They made desperate efforts to get along, but ever got more and more bogged—evidently the glide had vanished. When we got away we soon discovered how awful the surface had become; added to the forenoon difficulties the snow had become wet and sticky. We got our load along, soon passing Bowers, but the toil was simply awful. We were soaked with perspiration and thoroughly breathless with our efforts. Again and again the sledge got one runner on harder snow than the other, fell over on its side, and refused to move. At the top of the rise I found Evans reduced to relay work, and Bowers followed his example soon after. We got our whole load through till 7 P.M., camping time, but only with repeated

* Meares and the dog teams turned back on December 11.

halts and labour which was altogether too strenuous. The other parties certainly cannot get a full load along on the surface, and I much doubt if we could continue to do so, but we must try again to-morrow.

I suppose we have advanced a bare 4 miles to-day and the aspect of things is very little changed. Our height is now about 1,500 feet; I had pinned my faith on getting better conditions as we rose, but it looks as though matters were getting worse instead of better. As far as the Cloud-maker* the valley looks like a huge basin for the lodgment of such snow as this. We can but toil on, but it is woefully disheartening. I am not at all hungry, but pretty thirsty. (T. + 15°.) I find our summit ration† is even too filling for the present. Two skuas came round at lunch time, no doubt attracted by our 'Shambles' camp.

*Sunday, December 17.*—Camp 39. We got fearfully hot this morning and marched in singlets, which became wringing wet; thus uncovered the sun gets at one's skin, and then the wind, which makes it horribly uncomfortable. Our lips are very sore. We cover them with the soft silk plaster which seems about the best thing for the purpose.

I'm inclined to think that the summit trouble will be mostly due to the chill falling on sunburned skins. Even now one feels the cold strike directly one stops. We get fearfully thirsty and chip up ice on the march, as well as drinking a great deal of water on halting. Our fuel only just does it, but that is all we want, and we have a bit in hand for the summit.

The pulling this afternoon was fairly pleasant; at first over hard snow, and then on to pretty rough ice with surface

* A mountain nearly 10,000 feet high. *See* Map.
† The daily allowance of food for the summit of the plateau.

snow-filled cracks, bad for sledges, but ours promised to
come through well. We have worn our crampons all day
and are delighted with them. P.O. Evans, the inventor of
both crampons and ski shoes, is greatly pleased, and
certainly we owe him much. The weather is beginning to
look dirty again, snow clouds rolling in from the east
as usual. I believe it will be overcast to-morrow.

*Wednesday, December 20.*—Camp 42. 6,500 feet about.
Just got off our best half march—10 miles 1150 yards (geo.),
over 12 miles stat. With an afternoon to follow we should
do well to-day; the wind has been coming up the valley.
Turning this book* seems to have brought luck. We
marched on till nearly 7 o'clock after a long lunch halt, and
covered 19½ geo. miles, nearly 23 (stat.), rising 800 feet.
This morning we came over a considerable extent of hard
snow, then got to hard ice with patches of snow: a state of
affairs which has continued all day. Pulling the sledges in
crampons is no difficulty at all. At lunch Wilson and Bowers
walked back 2 miles or so to try and find Bowers' broken
sledgemeter, without result. During their absence a fog
spread about us, carried up the valleys by easterly wind.
We started the afternoon march in this fog very unpleasant-
ly, but later it gradually drifted, and to-night it is very fine
and warm. As the fog lifted we saw a huge line of pressure
ahead; I steered for a place where the slope looked
smoother, and we are camped beneath this spot to-night.
(Lat. 84′ 59′ 6″.) We must be ahead of Shackleton's position
on the 17th. All day we have been admiring the wonderful
banded structure of the rock; to-night it is beautifully clear
on Mount Darwin.†

* In the pocket journal, only one side of each page had been written
on. Coming to the end of it, Scott reversed the book, and continued
his entries on the empty backs of the pages.

† Near the top of the pass. *See* Map.

I have just told off the people to return to-morrow night: Atkinson, Wright, Cherry-Garrard, and Keohane. All are disappointed—poor Wright rather bitterly, I fear. I dreaded this necessity of choosing—nothing could be more heartrending. I calculated our programme to start from 85° 10′ with 12 units of food* and eight men. We ought to be in this position to-morrow night, less one day's food. After all our harassing trouble one cannot but be satisfied with such a prospect.

*Thursday, December 21.*—Camp 43. 'December 21, 1911. Lat. 85° S. We are struggling on, considering all things, against odds. The weather is a constant anxiety, otherwise arrangements are working exactly as planned.

'For your own ear also, I am exceedingly fit and can go with the best of them.

'It is a pity the luck doesn't come our way, because every detail of equipment is right.

'I write this sitting in our tent waiting for the fog to clear—an exasperating position as we are in the worst crevassed† region. Teddy Evans and Atkinson were down to the length of their harness this morning, and we have all been half-way down. As first man I get first chance, and it's decidedly exciting not knowing which step will give way. Still all this is interesting enough if one could only go on.

'Since writing the above I made a dash for it, got out of the valley, out of the fog, and away from crevasses. So here we are practically on the summit and up to date in the provision line. We ought to get through.'

* A unit of food means a week's supplies for four men.
† Crevasse—a deep crack in the ice surface.

# 13

# The Summit Journey to the Pole

*Monday, December 25*, CHRISTMAS.—Lunch. Bar. 21·14. Rise 240 feet. The wind was strong last night and this morning; a light snowfall in the night; a good deal of drift, subsiding when we started, but still about a foot high. I thought it might have spoilt the surface, but for the first hour and a half we went along in fine style. Then we started up a rise, and to our annoyance found ourselves amongst crevasses once more—very hard, smooth névé* between high ridges at the edge of crevasses, and therefore very difficult to get foothold to pull the sledges. Got our ski sticks out, which improved matters, but we had to tack a good deal and several of us went half down. After half an hour of this I looked round and found the second sledge halted some way in rear—evidently some one had gone into a crevasse. We saw the rescue work going on, but had to wait half an hour for the party to come up, and got mightily cold. It appears that Lashly went down very suddenly, nearly dragging the crew with him. The sledge ran on and jammed the span so that the Alpine rope had to be got out and used to pull Lashly to the surface again. Lashly says the crevasse was 50 feet deep and 8 feet across, in form U, showing that the word 'unfathomable' can rarely be applied. Lashly is 44 to-day and as hard as nails.

After topping the crevasse ridge we got on a better

* Hard frozen snow.

surface and came along fairly well, completing over 7 miles (geo.) just before 1 o'clock. We have risen nearly 250 feet this morning; the wind was strong and therefore trying, mainly because it held the sledge; it is a little lighter now.

Night camp No. 47. Bar. 21·18. T. −7°. I am so full up that I can scarcely write. After sundry luxuries, such as chocolate and raisins at lunch, we started off well, but soon got amongst crevasses, huge snow-filled roadways running almost in our direction, and across hidden cracks into which we frequently fell. Passing for two miles or so along between two roadways, we came on a huge pit with raised sides. Is this a submerged mountain peak or a swirl in the stream? Getting clear of crevasses and on a slightly down grade, we came along at a swinging pace—splendid. I marched on till nearly 7.30, when we had covered 15 miles (geo.) (17¼ stat.). I knew that supper was to be a 'tightener,' and indeed it has been—so much that I must leave description till the morning.

Dead reckoning, Lat. 85° 50′ S.; Long. 159° 8′ 2″ E. Bar. 21·22.

I must write a word of our supper last night. We had four courses. The first, pemmican,* full whack with slices of horse meat flavoured with onion and curry powder and thickened with biscuit; then an arrowroot, cocoa and biscuit hoosh† sweetened; then a plum-pudding; then cocoa with raisins, and finally a dessert of caramels and ginger. After the feast it was difficult to move. Wilson and I couldn't finish our share of plum-pudding. We have all slept splendidly and feel thoroughly warm—such is the effect of full feeding.

* Lean meat, closely compressed.
† Thick soup.

*Sunday, December 31.*—New Year's Eve. 20·17. Height about 9,126. T. − 10°. The second party left in depôt its ski and some other weights equivalent to about 100 lbs. I sent them off first; they marched, but not very fast. We followed and did not catch them before they camped by direction at 1.30 By this time we had covered exactly 7 miles (geo.), and we must have risen a good deal. We rose on one steep incline at the beginning of the march, and topped another at the end, showing a distance of about 5 miles between these wretched slopes which give us the hardest pulling, but as a matter of fact, we have been rising all day.

We had a good full brew of tea and then set to work stripping the sledges. That didn't take long, but the building up the 10-feet sledges is a long job. Evans (P.O.) and Crean are tackling it, and it is a very remarkable piece of work. To build a sledge under these conditions is a fact for special record. Evans (Lieut.) has just found the latitude—86° 56′ S., so that we are pretty near the 87th parallel aimed at for to-night. We lose half a day, but I hope to make that up by going forward at much better speed.

This is to be called the '3 Degree Depôt,' and it holds a week's provision for both units.

There is extraordinarily little mirage* up here and the refraction is very small. Except for the seamen we are all sitting in a double tent—the first time we have put up the inner lining to the tent; it seems to make us much snugger.

10 P.M.—The job of rebuilding is taking longer than I expected, but is now almost done. The 10-feet sledges

---

* Refraction, a change of direction in rays of light, causes mirage, an optical illusion in which objects are seen in impossible positions.

look very handy. We had an extra drink of tea and are now turned into our bags in the double tent (five of us) as warm as toast, and just enough light to write or work with. Did not get to bed till 2 A.M.

*Monday, January 1, 1912.*—NEW YEAR'S DAY. Lunch. Bar. 20·04. Roused hands about 7.30 and got away 9.30, Evans' party going ahead on foot. We followed on ski. Very stupidly we had not seen to our ski shoes beforehand, and it took a good half-hour to get them right; Wilson especially had trouble. When we did get away, to our surprise the sledge pulled very easily, and we made fine progress, rapidly gaining on the foot-haulers.

Night camp 54. Bar. 19·98. Risen about 150 feet. Height about 9,600 above Barrier. They camped for lunch at 5½ miles and went on early, completing 11·3 (geo.) by 7.30. We were delayed again at lunch camp, P.O. Evans repairing the tent, and I the cooker. We caught the other party more easily in the afternoon and kept alongside them the last quarter of an hour. It was surprising how easily the sledge pulled; we have scarcely exerted ourselves all day.

We have been rising again all day, but the slopes are less accentuated. I had expected trouble with ski and hard patches, but we found none at all. (T. −14°.) The temperature is steadily falling, but it seems to fall with the wind. We are *very* comfortable in our double tent. Stick of chocolate to celebrate the New Year. The supporting party not in very high spirits, they have not managed matters well for themselves. Prospects seem to get brighter —only 170 miles to go and plenty of food left.

*Thursday, January 4.*—We were naturally late getting away this morning, the sledge having to be packed and arrangements completed for separation of parties. It is wonderful to see how neatly everything stows on a little sledge, thanks to P.O. Evans. I was anxious to see how we could pull it, and glad to find we went easy enough. Bowers on foot pulls between, but behind, Wilson and myself; he has to keep his own pace and luckily does not throw us out at all.

The second party had followed us in case of accident, but as soon as I was certain we could get along we stopped and said farewell. Teddy Evans is terribly disappointed, but has taken it very well and behaved like a man. Poor old Crean wept and even Lashly was affected. I was glad to find their sledge is a mere nothing to them, and thus, no doubt, they will make a quick journey back. Since leaving them we have marched on till 1.15 and covered 6·2 miles (geo.). With full marching days we ought to have no difficulty in keeping up our average.*

Night camp 57. T. −16°. Height 10,280.—We started well on the afternoon march, going a good speed for $1\frac{1}{2}$ hours; then we came on a surface covered with loose sandy snow, and the pulling became very heavy. We managed to get off $12\frac{1}{2}$ miles (geo.) by 7 P.M., but it was very heavy work.

*Friday, January 5.*—Camp 58. We go little over a mile and a quarter an hour now—it is a big strain as the shadows creep slowly round from our right through ahead to our left. What lots of things we think of on these monotonous marches! What castles one builds now hopefully that the Pole is ours! Bowers took sights to-day and will take them every third day. We feel the cold very little, the great comfort of our situation is the excellent drying effect of the

* The final party for the Pole consisted of Scott, Wilson, Oates, Bowers and P.O. Evans.

sun. Our socks and finnesko are almost dry each morning. Cooking for five takes a seriously longer time than cooking for four; perhaps half an hour on the whole day. It is an item I had not considered when reorganising.*

*Monday, January 8.*—Noon. T. −19·8°. Min. for night −25°. Our first summit blizzard. We might just have started after breakfast, but the wind seemed obviously on the increase, and so it has proved. The sun has not been obscured, but snow is evidently falling as well as drifting. The sun seems to be getting a little brighter as the wind increases. The whole phenomenon is very like a Barrier blizzard, only there is much less snow, as one would expect, and at present less wind, which is somewhat of a surprise.

Evans' hand was dressed† this morning, and the rest ought to be good for it. I am not sure it will not do us all good as we lie, in our comfortable bags, within our double-walled tent. However, we do not want more than a day's delay, both on account of lost time and food and the slow accumulation of ice. (Night T. −13·5°.) It has grown much thicker during the day, from time to time obscuring the sun for the first time. The temperature is low for a blizzard, but the cold snow is not sticky and not easily carried into the tent, so that the sleeping-bags remain in good condition. (T. −3°.) The glass is rising slightly. I hope we shall be able to start in the morning.

It is quite impossible to speak too highly of my companions. Each fulfils his office to the party; Wilson, first as doctor, ever on the look out to alleviate the small pains and troubles incidental to the work; now as cook, quick, careful and dexterous, ever thinking of some fresh expedient

* When he sent back the three extra men.
† He had cut it the day before, while sledge-making.

to help the camp life; tough as steel on the traces, never wavering from start to finish.

Evans, a giant worker with a really remarkable headpiece. It is only now I realise how much has been due to him. Our ski shoes and crampons have been absolutely indispensable, and if the original ideas were not his, the details of manufacture and design and the good workmanship are his alone. He is responsible for every sledge, every sledge fitting, tents, sleeping-bags, harness, and when one cannot recall a single expression of dissatisfaction with any one of these items, it shows what an invaluable assistant he has been. Now, besides superintending the putting up of the tent, he thinks out and arranges the packing of the sledge; it is extraordinary how neatly and handily everything is stowed, and how much study has been given to preserving the suppleness and good running qualities of the machine. On the Barrier, before the ponies were killed, he was ever roaming round, correcting faults of stowage.

Little Bowers remains a marvel—he is thoroughly enjoying himself. I leave all the provision arrangement in his hands, and at all times he knows exactly how we stand, or how each returning party should fare. It has been a complicated business to re-distribute stores at various stages of re-organisation, but not one single mistake has been made. In addition to the stores, he keeps the most thorough and conscientious meteorological record, and to this he now adds the duty of observer and photographer. Nothing comes amiss to him, and no work is too hard. It is a difficulty to get him into the tent; he seems quite oblivious of the cold, and he lies coiled in his bag writing and working out sights long after the others are asleep.

Of these three it is a matter for thought and congratulation that each is specially suited for his own work, but would not be capable of doing that of the others as well as it is done. Each is invaluable. Oates had his invaluable period with the ponies; now he is a foot slogger and goes hard the whole time, does his share of camp work, and stands the hardship as well as any of us. I would not like to be without him either. So our five people are perhaps as happily selected as it is possible to imagine.

*Thursday, January 11.*—Night. Height 10,530. Temp. −16·3°. Minimum −25·8°. Another hard grind in the afternoon and five miles added. About 74 miles from the Pole—can we keep this up for seven days? It takes it out of us like anything. None of us ever had such hard work before. Cloud has been coming and going overhead all day, drifting from the S.E., but continually altering shape. Snow crystals falling all the time; a very light S. breeze at start soon dying away. The sun so bright and warm to-night that it is almost impossible to imagine a minus temperature. The snow seems to get softer as we advance; the sastrugi, though sometimes high and undercut, are not hard—no crusts, except yesterday the surface subsided once, as on the Barrier. Our chance still holds good if we can put the work in, but it's a terribly trying time.

*Saturday, January 13.*—Only 51 miles from the Pole to-night. If we don't get to it we shall be very close. There is a little southerly breeze to-night; I devoutly hope it may increase in force. The alternation of soft snow and sastrugi seems to suggest that the coastal mountains are not so very far away.

*Sunday, January 14.*—Camp 66. Lunch T. −18°, Night T. −15°. Sun showing mistily through overcast sky all day. Light southerly wind with very low drift. In

One of the motor sledges

The polar party: on the trail (Evans, Oates, Wilson, Scott)

Ponies on the march

A dog team and sledge

consequence the surface was a little better, and we came along very steadily 6·3 miles in the morning and 5·5 in the afternoon, but the steering was awfully difficult and trying; very often I could see nothing, and Bowers in my shadow directed me. Under such circumstances it is an immense help to be pulling on ski. To-night it is looking very thick. The sun can barely be distinguished, the temperature has risen, and there are serious indications of a blizzard. I trust they will not come to anything; there are practically no signs of heavy wind here, so that even if it blows a little we may be able to march. Meanwhile we are less than 40 miles from the Pole.

Again we noticed the cold; at lunch to-day (Obs.: Lat. 89° 20′ 53″ S.) all our feet were cold, but this was mainly due to the bald state of our finnesko.* I put some grease under the bare skin and found it made all the difference. Oates seems to be feeling the cold and fatigue more than the rest of us, but we are all very fit. It is a critical time, but we ought to pull through. The barometer has fallen considerably. Oh! for a few fine days! So close it seems and only the weather to baulk us.

*Night, January 15.*—It is wonderful to think that two long marches would land us at the Pole. We left our depôt to-day with nine days' provisions, so that it ought to be a certain thing now, and the only appalling possibility the sight of the Norwegian flag forestalling ours. Little Bowers continues his indefatigable efforts to get good sights, and it is wonderful how he works them up in his sleeping-bag in our congested tent. (Minimum for night −27·5°.) Only 27 miles from the Pole. We *ought* to do it now.

*Tuesday, January 16.*—Camp 68. Height 9,760. T. −23·5°. The worst has happened, or nearly the worst. We

* Fur boots.

10

marched well in the morning and covered 7½ miles. Noon sight showed us in Lat. 89° 42′ S., and we started off in high spirits in the afternoon, feeling that to-morrow would see us at our destination. About the second hour of the march Bowers' sharp eyes detected what he thought was a cairn; he was uneasy about it, but argued that it must be a sastrugus. Half an hour later he detected a black speck ahead. Soon we knew that this could not be a natural snow feature. We marched on, found that it was a black flag tied to a sledge bearer; near by the remains of a camp; sledge tracks and ski tracks going and coming and the clear trace of dogs' paws—many dogs. This told us the whole story. The Norwegians have forestalled us and are first at the Pole. It is a terrible disappointment, and I am very sorry for my loyal companions. Many thoughts come and much discussion have we had. To-morrow we must march on to the Pole and then hasten home with all the speed we can compass. All the day-dreams must go; it will be a wearisome return. Certainly we are descending in altitude—certainly also the Norwegians found an easy way up.

*Wednesday, January 17.*—Camp 69. T. −22° at start. Night −21°. The Pole. Yes, but under very different circumstances from those expected. We have had a horrible day—add to our disappointment a head wind 4 to 5,* with a temperature −22°, and companions labouring on with cold feet and hands.

We started at 7.30, none of us having slept much after the shock of our discovery. We followed the Norwegian sledge tracks for some way; as far as we make out there are only two men. In about three miles we passed two small cairns. Then the weather overcast, and the tracks being

* Half a gale. The velocity of wind is denoted by numbers (1–10).

increasingly drifted up and obviously going too far to the west, we decided to make straight for the Pole according to our calculations. At 12.30 Evans had such cold hands we camped for lunch—an excellent 'week-end' one. We had marched 7·4 miles. Lat. sight gave 89° 53′ 37″. We started out and did 6½ miles due south. To-night little Bowers is laying himself out to get sights in terrible difficult circumstances; the wind is blowing hard, T. −21°, and there is that curious damp, cold feeling in the air which chills one to the bone in no time. We have been descending again, I think, but there looks to be a rise ahead; otherwise there is very little that is different from the awful monotony of past days. Great God! this is an awful place and terrible enough for us to have laboured to it without the reward of priority. Well, it is something to have got here, and the wind may be our friend to-morrow. We have had a fat Polar hoosh in spite of our chagrin, and feel comfortable inside—added a small stick of chocolate and the queer taste of a cigarette brought by Wilson. Now for the run home and a desperate struggle. I wonder if we can do it.

*Thursday morning, January 18.*—Decided after summing up all observations that we were 3·5 miles away from the Pole—one mile beyond it and 3 to the right. More or less in this direction Bowers saw a cairn or tent.

We have just arrived at this tent, 2 miles from our camp, therefore about 1½ miles from the Pole. In the tent we find a record of five Norwegians having been here, as follows:

> Roald Amundsen
> Olav Olavson Bjaaland
> Hilmer Hanssen
> Sverre H. Hassel
> Oscar Wisting.     16 Dec. 1911.

The tent is fine—a small compact affair supported by a single bamboo. A note from Amundsen, which I keep, asks me to forward a letter to King Haakon!*

The following articles have been left in the tent: 3 half bags of reindeer containing a miscellaneous assortment of mits and sleeping socks, very various in description, a sextant, a Norwegian artificial horizon and a hypsometer without boiling-point thermometers, a sextant and hypsometer† of English make.

Left a note to say I had visited the tent with companions; Bowers photographing and Wilson sketching. Since lunch we have marched 6·2 miles S.S.E. by compass (i.e. northwards). Sights at lunch gave us ½ to ¾ of a mile from the Pole, so we call it the Pole Camp. (Temp. Lunch −21°.) We built a cairn, put up our poor slighted Union Jack, and photographed ourselves—mighty cold work all of it— less than ½ a mile south we saw stuck up an old underrunner of a sledge. This we commandeered as a yard for a floorcloth sail.‡ I imagine it was intended to mark the exact spot of the Pole as near as the Norwegians could fix it. (Height 9,500.) A note attached talked of the tent as being 2 miles from the Pole. Wilson keeps the note. There is no doubt that our predecessors have made thoroughly sure of their mark and fully carried out their programme. I think the Pole is about 9,500 feet in height; this is remarkable, considering that in Lat. 88° we were about 10,500.

We carried the Union Jack about ¾ of a mile north with us and left it on a piece of stick as near as we could fix it. I fancy the Norwegians arrived at the pole on the 15th Dec.

---

\* Of Norway, Amundsen's country.
† An instrument for measuring height.
‡ To help the sledge along.

and left on the 17th, ahead of a date quoted by me in London as ideal, viz. Dec. 22. It looks as though the Norwegian party expected colder weather on the summit than they got; it could scarcely be otherwise from Shackleton's account. Well, we have turned our back now on the goal of our ambition and must face our 800 miles of solid dragging—and good-bye to most of the day-dreams!

# 14

# The Return from the Pole

*Friday, January 19.*—Lunch 8·1 miles, T. −20·6°. Early in the march we picked up a Norwegian cairn and our outward tracks. We followed these to the ominous black flag which had first apprised us of our predecessors' success. We have picked this flag up, using the staff for our sail, and are now camped about 1½ miles further back on our tracks. So that is the last of the Norwegians for the present. The surface undulates considerably about this latitude; it was more evident to-day than when we were outward bound.

It is warmer and pleasanter marching with the wind, but I'm not sure we don't feel the cold more when we stop and camp than we did on the outward march. We pick up our cairns easily, and ought to do so right through, I think; but, of course, one will be a bit anxious till the Three Degree Depôt is reached.* I'm afraid the return journey is going to be dreadfully tiring and monotonous.

*Sunday, January 21.*—R. 4: 10,010.† Temp. blizzard, −18° to −11°, to −14° now. Awoke to a stiff blizzard; air very thick with snow and sun very dim. We decided not to march owing to likelihood of losing track; expected at least a day of lay up, but whilst at lunch there was a sudden

---

* Still over 150 miles away. They had marched 7 miles on the homeward track the first afternoon, 18½ the second day.

† R. 4 means 4th camp on return journey; 10,010 is the height.

clearance and wind dropped to light breeze. We got ready to march, but gear was so iced up we did not get away till 3.45. Marched till 7.40—a terribly weary four-hour drag; even with helping wind we only did $5\frac{1}{2}$ miles ($6\frac{1}{4}$ statute). The surface bad, horribly bad on new sastrugi, and decidedly rising again in elevation.

We are going to have a pretty hard time this next 100 miles, I expect. If it was difficult to drag down-hill over this belt, it will probably be a good deal more difficult to drag up. Luckily the tracks are fairly distinct, though we only see our cairns when less than a mile away; 45 miles to the next depôt and 6 days' food in hand—then pick up 7 days' food (T. $-22°$) and 90 miles to go to the 'Three Degree' Depôt. Once there we ought to be safe, but we ought to have a day or two in hand on arrival and may have difficulty with following the tracks. However, if we can get a rating sight* for our watches to-morrow we should be independent of the tracks at a pinch.

*Monday, January 22.*—10,000. Temp. $-21°$. I think about the most tiring march we have had; solid pulling the whole way, in spite of the light sledge and some little helping wind at first. Then in the last part of the afternoon the sun came out, and almost immediately we had the whole surface covered with soft snow.

We got away sharp at 8 and marched a solid 9 hours, and thus we have covered 14·5 miles (geo.) but, by Jove! it has been a grind. We are just about on the 89th parallel. To-night Bowers got a rating sight. We are within $2\frac{1}{2}$ miles of the 64th camp cairn, 30 miles from our depôt, and with 5 days' food in hand. Ski boots are beginning to show signs of wear; I trust we shall have no giving out of ski or boots,

* An observation of the sun, to fix the time of the chronometers.

since there are yet so many miles to go. I thought we were climbing to-day, but the barometer* gives no change.

*Tuesday, January 23.*—Lowest Minimum last night − 30°, Temp. at start − 28°. Lunch height 10,100. Temp. with wind 6 to 7, − 19°. Little wind and heavy marching at start. Then wind increased and we did 8·7 miles by lunch, when it was practically blowing a blizzard. The old tracks show so remarkably well that we can follow them without much difficulty—a great piece of luck.

In the afternoon we had to reorganise. Could carry a whole sail. Bowers hung on to the sledge, Evans and Oates had to lengthen out. We came along at a great rate and should have got within an easy march of our depôt had not Wilson suddenly discovered that Evans' nose was frostbitten —it was white and hard. We thought it best to camp at 6.45. Got the tent up with some difficulty, and now pretty cosy after good hoosh.

There is no doubt Evans is a good deal run down—his fingers are badly blistered and his nose is rather seriously congested with frequent frost-bites. He is very much annoyed with himself, which is not a good sign. I think Wilson, Bowers and I are as fit as possible under the circumstances. Oates gets cold feet. One way and another, I shall be glad to get off the summit! We are only about 13 miles from our 'Degree and half' Depôt, and should get there to-morrow. The weather seems to be breaking up. Pray God we have something of a track to follow to the Three Degree Depôt—once we pick that up we ought to be right.

*Thursday, January 25.*—Temp. Lunch − 11°, Temp.

* Changes of altitude are indicated by the barometer's rise or fall.

night − 16°. Thank God we found our Half Degree Depôt. After lying in our bags yesterday afternoon and all night, we debated breakfast; decided to have it later and go without lunch. At the time the gale seemed as bad as ever, but during breakfast the sun showed and there was light enough to see the old track. It was a long and terribly cold job digging out our sledge and breaking camp, but we got through and on the march without sail, all pulling. This was about 11, and at about 2.30, to our joy, we saw the red depôt flag. We had lunch and left with 9½ days' provisions, still following the track—marched till 8 and covered over 5 miles, over 12 in the day. Only 89 miles (geogr.) to the next depôt, but it's time we cleared off this plateau. We are not without ailments: Oates suffers from a very cold foot; Evans' fingers and nose are in a bad state, and to-night Wilson is suffering tortures from his eyes. Bowers and I are the only members of the party without troubles just at present. The weather still looks unsettled, and I fear a succession of blizzards at this time of year; the wind is strong from the south, and this afternoon has been very helpful with the full sail. Needless to say I shall sleep much better with our provision bag full again. The only real anxiety now is the finding of the Three Degree Depôt. The tracks seem as good as ever so far; sometimes for 30 or 40 yards we lose them under drifts, but then they reappear quite clearly raised above the surface. If the light is good there is not the least difficulty in following. Blizzards are our bugbear, not only stopping our marches, but the cold damp air takes it out of us. Bowers got another rating sight to-night—it was wonderful how he managed to observe in such a horribly cold wind.

*Saturday, January 27.*—R. 10. Temp. − 16° (lunch),

— 14·3° (evening). Minimum — 19°. Height 9,900. Barometer low?* Called the hands half an hour late, but we got away in good time. The forenoon march was over the belt of storm-tossed sastrugi; it looked liked a rough sea. Wilson and I pulled in front on ski, the remainder on foot. It was very tricky work following the track, which pretty constantly disappeared, and in fact only showed itself by faint signs anywhere—a foot or two of raised sledge-track, a dozen yards of the trail of the sledgemeter wheel, or a spatter of hard snow-flicks where feet had trodden. Sometimes none of these were distinct, but one got an impression of lines which guided. The trouble was that on the outward track one had to shape course constantly to avoid the heaviest mounds, and consequently there were many zigzags. We lost a good deal over a mile by these halts, in which we unharnessed and went on the search for signs. However, by hook or by crook, we managed to stick on the old track. Came on the cairn quite suddenly, marched past it, and camped for lunch at 7 miles. In the afternoon the sastrugi gradually diminished in size and now we are on fairly level ground to-day, the obstruction practically at an end, and, to our joy, the tracks showing up much plainer again. For the last two hours we had no difficulty at all in following them. There has been a nice helpful southerly breeze all day, a clear sky and comparatively warm temperature. The air is dry again, so that tents and equipment are gradually losing their icy condition.

Our sleeping-bags are slowly but surely getting wetter and I'm afraid it will take a lot of this weather to put them right. However, we all sleep well enough in them, the

* Scott evidently thinks the height as indicated by the barometer may be wrong.

hours allowed being now on the short side. We are slowly getting more hungry, and it would be an advantage to have a little more food, especially for lunch. If we get to the next depôt in a few marches (it is now less than 60 miles and we have a full week's food) we ought to be able to open out a little, but we can't look for a real feed till we get to the pony food depôt. A long way to go, and, by Jove, this is tremendous labour.

*Sunday, January 28.*—Three articles were dropped on our outward march—Oates' pipe, Bowers' fur mits, and Evans' night boots. We picked up the boots and mits on the track, and to-night we found the pipe lying placidly in sight on the snow. The sledge tracks were very easy to follow to-day; they are becoming more and more raised, giving a good line shadow often visible half a mile ahead. If this goes on and the weather holds we shall get our depôt without trouble. I shall indeed be glad to get it* on the sledge. We are getting more hungry, there is no doubt. The lunch meal is beginning to seem inadequate. We are pretty thin, especially Evans, but none of us are feeling worked out. I doubt if we could drag heavy loads, but we can keep going well with our light one. We talk of food a good deal more, and shall be glad to open out on it.

*Monday, January 29.*—R. 12. Lunch Temp. −23°. Supper Temp. −25°. Height 10,000. Excellent march of 19½ miles, 10·5 before lunch. Wind helping greatly; considerable drift; tracks for the most part very plain. Some time before lunch we picked up the return track of the supporting party, so that there are now three distinct sledge impressions. We are only 24 miles from our depôt—an easy day and a half. Given a fine day to-morrow we ought to get it

* *I.e.* the store of provisions.

without difficulty. The wind and sastrugi are S.S.E. and S.E. If the weather holds we ought to do the rest of the inland ice journey in little over a week. The surface is very much altered since we passed out. The loose snow has been swept into heaps, hard and wind-tossed. The rest has a glazed appearance, the loose drifting snow no doubt acting on it, polishing it like a sand blast. The sledge with our good wind behind runs splendidly on it; it is all soft and sandy beneath the glaze We are certainly getting hungrier every day. The day after to-morrow we should be able to increase allowances. It is monotonous work, but, thank God, the miles are coming fast at last. We ought not to be delayed much now with the down-grade in front of us.

*Tuesday, January 30.*—R. 13. 9,860. Lunch Temp. −25°, Supper Temp. −24·5°. Thank the Lord, another fine march—19 miles. We have passed the last cairn before the depôt, the track is clear ahead, the weather fair, the wind helpful, the gradient down—with any luck we should pick up our depôt in the middle of the morning march. This is the bright side; the reverse of the medal is serious. Wilson has strained a tendon in his leg; it has given pain all day and is swollen to-night. Of course, he is full of pluck over it, but I don't like the idea of such an accident here. To add to the trouble Evans has dislodged two finger-nails to-night; his hands are really bad, and to my surprise he shows signs of losing heart over it. He hasn't been cheerful since the accident.* The wind shifted from S.E. to S. and back again all day, but luckily it keeps strong. We can get along with bad fingers, but it [will be] a mighty serious thing if Wilson's leg doesn't improve.

*Sunday, February 4.*—R. 18. 8,620 feet. Temp.: Lunch

* *See* p. 124.

− 22°; Supper − 23°. Pulled on foot in the morning over good hard surface and covered 9·7 miles. Just before lunch unexpectedly fell into crevasses, Evans and I together—a second fall for Evans—and I camped. After lunch saw disturbance ahead, and what I took for disturbance (land) to the right. We went on ski over hard shiny descending surface. Did very well, especially towards end of march, covering in all 18·1. We have come down some hundreds of feet. Half way in the march the land showed up splendidly, and I decided to make straight for Mt. Darwin, which we are rounding. Every sign points to getting away off this plateau. The temperature is 20° lower than when we were here before; the party is not improving in condition, especially Evans, who is becoming rather dull and incapable.* Thank the Lord, we have good food at each meal, but we get hungrier in spite of it. Bowers is splendid, full of energy and bustle all the time. I hope we are not going to have trouble with ice-falls.

*Tuesday, February 6.*—Lunch 7,900; Supper 7,210. Temp. − 15° [R. 20]. We've had a horrid day and not covered good mileage. On turning out found sky overcast; a beastly position amidst crevasses. Luckily it cleared just before we started. We went straight for Mt. Darwin, but in half an hour found ourselves amongst huge open chasms, unbridged, but not very deep, I think. We turned to the north between two, but to our chagrin they converged into chaotic disturbance. We had to retrace our steps for a mile or so, then struck to the west and got on to a confused sea of sastrugi, pulling very hard; we put up the sail, Evans' nose suffered, Wilson very cold, everything horrid. Camped for lunch in the sastrugi; the only comfort, things looked

* The result of concussion in the morning's fall.

clearer to the west and we were obviously going downhill. In the afternoon we struggled on, got out of sastrugi and turned over on glazed surface, crossing many crevasses— very easy work on ski. Towards the end of the march we realised the certainty of maintaining a more or less straight course to the depôt, and estimate distance 10 to 15 miles.

Food is low and weather uncertain, so that many hours of the day were anxious; but this evening, though we are not as far advanced as I expected, the outlook is much more promising. Evans is the chief anxiety now; his cuts and wounds suppurate, his nose looks very bad, and altogether he shows considerable signs of being played out. Things may mend for him on the glacier, and his wounds get some respite under warmer conditions. I am indeed glad to think we shall so soon have done with plateau conditions. It took us 27 days to reach the Pole and 21 days back—in all 48 days—nearly 7 weeks in low temperature with almost incessant wind.

## END OF THE SUMMIT JOURNEY

*Wednesday, February 7.*—Mount Darwin [or Upper Glacier] Depôt, R. 21. Height 7,100. Lunch Temp. −9°; Supper Temp. [a blank here]. A wretched day with satisfactory ending. First panic, certainty that biscuit-box was short. Great doubt as to how this has come about, as we certainly haven't over-issued allowances. Bowers is dreadfully disturbed about it. The shortage is a full day's allowance. We started our march at 8.30, and travelled down slopes and over terraces covered with hard sastrugi— very tiresome work—and the land didn't seem to come any nearer. At lunch the wind increased, and what with hot tea and good food, we started the afternoon in a better frame of mind, and it soon became obvious we were nearing our mark. Soon after 6.30 we saw our depôt easily and camped next it at 7.30.

Found note from E. Evans to say the second return party passed through safely at 2.30 on January 14—half a day longer between depôts than we have been. The temperature is higher, but there is a cold wind to-night.

Well, we have come through our 7 weeks' ice camp journey and most of us are fit, but I think another week might have had a very bad effect on P.O. Evans, who is going steadily downhill.

It is satisfactory to recall that these facts give absolute proof of both expeditions having reached the Pole and placed the question of priority beyond discussion.

RETURN FROM FIRST SUMMIT DEPÔT

*Thursday, February 8.*—R. 22. Height 6260. Start Temp. −11°; Lunch Temp. −5°; Supper, zero. 9·2 miles. Started from the depôt rather late owing to weighing biscuit, &c., and rearranging matters. Had a beastly morning. Wind very strong and cold. Steered in for Mt. Darwin to visit rock. Sent Bowers on, on ski, as Wilson can't wear his at present. He obtained several specimens, all of much the same type, a close-grained granite rock which weathers red. Hence the pink lime-stone. After he rejoined we skidded downhill pretty fast, leaders on ski, Oates and Wilson on foot alongside sledge—Evans detached. We lunched at 2 well down towards Mt. Buckley, the wind half a gale and everybody very cold and cheerless. However, better things were to follow. We decided to steer for the moraine* under Mt. Buckley and, pulling with crampons, we crossed some very irregular steep slopes with big crevasses and slid down towards the rocks. The moraine was obviously so interesting that when we had advanced some miles and got out of the wind, I decided to camp and spend the rest of the day geologising. It has been extremely interesting. We found ourselves under perpendicular cliffs of Beacon sandstone, weathering rapidly and carrying veritable coal seams. From the last Wilson, with his sharp eyes, has picked several plant impressions, the last a piece of coal with beautifully traced leaves in layers, also some excellently preserved impressions of thick stems, showing cellular structure. In one place we saw the cast of small waves in the sand. To-night Bill has got a specimen of limestone with archeocyathus†—the trouble is one cannot imagine where the stone comes from; it is evidently rare, as few specimens occur in the moraine. There is a good deal of pure white quartz.‡ Altogether we have had a most interesting afternoon, and the relief of being out of the wind and in a warmer temperature is inexpressible. I hope and trust we shall all buck up again now that the conditions are more favourable. We have been in shadow all the afternoon, but the sun has just reached us, a little obscured by night haze. A lot could be written on the delight of setting foot on rock after 14 weeks of snow and ice and nearly 7 out of sight of aught else. It is like going ashore after a sea voyage. We deserve a little good bright weather after all our trials, and hope to get a chance to dry our

* A varied mass of rock, sand, &c., carried down by a glacier and piled up at the bottom.
† A fossil plant.
‡ A mineral in form of crystals.

Members of the polar party having a meal in camp. (Evans, Bowers, Wilson, Scott)

The polar party's sledging ration. (Pemmican, biscuits, butter, cocoa, sugar and tea)

Heavy pulling in deep snow on the Beardmore Glacier
Scott's party at Amundsen's tent

sleeping-bags and generally make our gear more comfortable.*

*Saturday, February 10.*—R. 24. Lunch Temp. +12°; Supper Temp. +10°. Got off a good morning march in spite of keeping too far east and getting in rough, cracked ice. Had a splendid night's sleep, showing great change in all faces, so didn't get away till 10 A.M. Lunched just before 3. After lunch the land began to be obscured. We held a course for 2½ hours with difficulty, then the sun disappeared, and snow drove in our faces with northerly wind —very warm and impossible to steer, so camped. After supper, still very thick all round, but sun showing and less snow falling. The fallen snow crystals are quite feathery like thistledown. We have two full days' food left, and though our position is uncertain, we are certainly within two outward marches from the middle glacier depôt. However, if the weather doesn't clear by to-morrow, we must either march blindly on or reduce food. It is very trying. Another night to make up arrears of sleep. The ice crystals that first fell this afternoon were very large. Now the sky is clearer overhead, the temperature has fallen slightly, and the crystals are minute.

*Sunday, February 11.*—R. 25. Lunch Temp. +6·5°; Supper +3·5°. The worst day we have had during the trip and greatly owing to our own fault. We started on a wretched surface with light S.W. wind, sail set, and pulling on ski—in a horrible light, which made everything look fantastic. As we went on the light got worse, and suddenly we found ourselves in pressure. Then came the fatal decision to steer east. We went on for 6 hours, hoping to do a good

* The fossils in these specimens proved to be the most valuable obtained by the Expedition.

11

distance, which in fact I suppose we did, but for the last hour or two we pressed on into a regular trap. Getting on to a good surface we did not reduce our lunch meal, and thought all going well, but half an hour after lunch we got into the worst ice mess I have ever been in. For three hours we plunged on on ski, first thinking we were too much to the right, then too much to the left; meanwhile the disturbance got worse and my spirits received a very rude shock. There were times when it seemed almost impossible to find a way out of the awful turmoil in which we found ourselves. At length, arguing that there must be a way on our left, we plunged in that direction. It got worse, harder, more icy and crevassed. We could not manage our ski and pulled on foot, falling into crevasses every minute—most luckily with no bad accident. At length we saw a smoother slope towards the land, pushed for it, but knew it was a woefully long way from us. The turmoil changed in character, irregular crevassed surface giving way to huge chasms, closely packed and most difficult to cross. It was very heavy work, but we had grown desperate. We won through at 10 P.M. and I write after 12 hours on the march. I *think* we are on or about the right track now, but we are still a good number of miles from the depôt, so we reduced rations to-night. We had three pemmican meals left and decided to make them into four. To-morrow's lunch must serve for two if we do not make big progress. It was a test of our endurance on the march and our fitness with small supper. We have come through well. A good wind has come down the glacier which is clearing the sky and surface. Pray God the wind holds to-morrow. Short sleep to-night and off first thing, I hope.

*Monday, February 12.*—R. 26. In a very critical situation.

All went well in the forenoon, and we did a good long march over a fair surface. Two hours before lunch we were cheered by the sight of our night camp of the 18th December, the day after we made our depôt—this showed we were on the right track. In the afternoon, refreshed by tea, we went forward, confident of covering the remaining distance, but by a fatal chance we kept too far to the left, and then we struck uphill and, tired and despondent, arrived in a horrid maze of crevasses and fissures. Divided counsels caused our course to be erratic after this, and finally, at 9 P.M., we landed in the worst place of all. After discussion we decided to camp, and here we are, after a very short supper and one meal only remaining in the food-bag; the depôt doubtful in locality. We *must* get there to-morrow. Meanwhile we are cheerful with an effort. It's a tight place, but luckily we've been well fed up to the present. Pray God we have fine weather to-morrow.

*Wednesday, February 14.*—There is no getting away from the fact that we are not pulling strong: probably none of us. Wilson's leg still troubles him and he doesn't like to trust himself on ski; but the worst case is Evans, who is giving us serious anxiety. This morning he suddenly disclosed a huge blister on his foot. It delayed us on the march, when he had to have his crampon readjusted. Sometimes I fear he is going from bad to worse, but I trust he will pick up again when we come to steady work on ski like this afternoon. He is hungry and so is Wilson. We can't risk opening out our food again, and as cook at present I am serving something under full allowance. We are inclined to get slack and slow with our camping arrangements, and small delays increase. I have talked of the matter tonight and hope for improvement. We cannot do distance without the hours. The next depôt* some 30 miles away and nearly 3 days' food in hand.

*Friday, February 16.*—12·5 m. Lunch Temp. +6·1°; Supper Temp. +7°. A rather trying position. Evans has nearly broken down in brain, we think. He is absolutely changed from his normal self-reliant self. This morning and this afternoon he stopped the march on some trivial excuse. We are on short rations, but not very short, food spins out till to-morrow night. We cannot be more than 10 or 12 miles from the depôt, but the weather is all against us. After lunch we were enveloped in a snow sheet, land just looming. Memory should hold the events of a very troublesome march with more troubles ahead. Perhaps all will be well if we can get to our depôt to-morrow fairly early, but it is anxious work with the sick man. But it's no use meeting troubles half way, and our sleep is all too short to write more.

*Saturday, February 17.*—A very terrible day. Evans looked a little better after a good sleep, and declared, as he always did, that he was quite well. He started in his place on the traces, but half an hour later worked his ski shoes adrift, and had to leave the sledge. The surface was awful, the soft recently fallen snow clogging the ski and runners at every step, the sledge groaning, the sky overcast, and the land hazy. We stopped after about one hour, and Evans came up again, but very slowly. Half an hour later he dropped out again on the same plea. He asked Bowers to lend him a piece of string. I cautioned him to come on as quickly as he could and he answered cheerfully as I thought. We had to push on, and the remainder of us were forced to pull very hard, sweating heavily. Abreast the

* The Lower Glacier Depôt.

Monument Rock we stopped, and seeing Evans a long way astern, I camped for lunch. There was no alarm at first, and we prepared tea and our own meal, consuming the latter. After lunch, and Evans still not appearing, we looked out, to see him still afar off. By this time we were alarmed, and all four started back on ski. I was first to reach the poor man and shocked at his appearance; he was on his knees with clothing disarranged, hands uncovered and frostbitten, and a wild look in his eyes. Asked what was the matter, he replied with a slow speech that he didn't know, but thought he must have fainted. We got him on his feet, but after two or three steps he sank down again. He showed every sign of complete collapse. Wilson, Bowers, and I went back for the sledge, whilst Oates remained with him. When we returned he was practically unconscious, and when we got him into the tent quite comatose.* He died quietly at 12.30 A.M. On discussing the symptoms we think he began to get weaker just before we reached the Pole, and that his downward path was accelerated first by the shock of his frostbitten fingers, and later by falls during rough travelling on the glacier, further by his loss of all confidence in himself. Wilson thinks it certain he must have injured his brain by a fall. It is a terrible thing to lose a companion in this way, but calm reflection shows that there could not have been a better ending to the terrible anxieties of the past week. Discussion of the situation at lunch yesterday shows us what a desperate pass we were in with a sick man on our hands so far from home.

At 1 A.M. we packed up and came down over the pressure ridges, finding our depôt easily.

* In state of coma, *i.e.* without sense or feeling.

# 15

# The Last March

*Monday, February 19**—R. 33. Temp. −17°. We have struggled out 4·6 miles in a short day over a really terrible surface—it has been like pulling over desert sand, without the least glide in the world. If this goes on we shall have a bad time, but I sincerely trust it is only the result of the windless area close to the coast and that, as we are making steadily outwards, we shall shortly escape it. It is perhaps premature to be anxious about covering distance. In all other respects things are improving. We have our sleeping-bags spread on the sledge and they are drying, but, above all, we have our full measure of food again. To-night we had a sort of stew fry of pemmican and horseflesh, and voted it the best hoosh we had ever had on a sledge journey. The absence of poor Evans is a help to the commissariat, but if he had been here in a fit state we might have got along faster. I wonder what is in store for us, with some little alarm at the lateness of the season.

[*Here follows a depressing record of a monotonous fortnight's progress.*]

*Friday, March 2.*—Lunch. Misfortunes rarely come singly. We marched to the [Middle Barrier] depôt fairly easily yesterday afternoon, and since that have suffered three distinct blows which have placed us in a bad position.

* At Shambles Camp on February 18 they had picked up a supply of horsemeat.

First we found a shortage of oil; with most rigid economy it can scarce carry us to the next depôt on this surface [71 miles away]. Second, Titus Oates disclosed his feet, the toes showing very bad indeed, evidently bitten by the late temperatures. The third blow came in the night, when the wind, which we had hailed with some joy, brought dark overcast weather. It fell below −40° in the night, and this morning it took 1½ hours to get our foot-gear on, but we got away before eight. We lost cairn and tracks together and made as steady as we could N. by W., but have seen nothing. Worse was to come—the surface is simply awful. In spite of strong wind and full sail we have only done 5½ miles. We are in a *very* queer street, since there is no doubt we cannot do the extra marches and feel the cold horribly.

*Sunday, March 4.*—Lunch. Things looking *very* black indeed. As usual we forgot our trouble last night, got into our bags, slept splendidly on good hoosh, woke and had another, and started marching. Sun shining brightly, tracks clear, but surface covered with sandy frost-rime. All the morning we had to pull with all our strength, and in 4½ hours we covered 3½ miles. Last night it was overcast and thick, surface bad; this morning sun shining and surface as bad as ever. Under the immediate surface crystals is a hard sastrugi surface, which must have been excellent for pulling a week or two ago. We are about 42 miles from the next depôt and have a week's food, but only about 3 to 4 days' fuel—we are as economical of the latter as one can possibly be, and we cannot afford to save food and pull as we are pulling. We are in a very tight place indeed, but none of us despondent *yet*, or at least we preserve every semblance of good cheer, but one's heart sinks as the sledge stops dead at some sastrugi behind which the surface sand lies thickly heaped. For the moment the temperature is in the −20°—an improvement which makes us much more comfortable, but a colder snap is bound to come again soon. I fear that Oates at least will weather such an event very poorly. Providence to our aid! We can expect little from man now except the possibility of extra food at the next depôt. It will be real bad if we get there and find the same shortage of oil. Shall we get there? Such a short distance it would have appeared to us on the summit! I don't know what I should do if Wilson and Bowers weren't so determinedly cheerful over things.

*Monday, March 5.*—Lunch. Regret to say going from bad to worse. We got a slant of wind yesterday afternoon, and going on 5 hours we converted our wretched morning run of 3½ miles into something over 9. We went to bed on a cup of cocoa and pemmican solid with the chill off. (R. 47.) The result is telling on all, but mainly on Oates, whose feet are in a wretched condition. One swelled up tremendously last night and he is very lame this morning. We started march on tea and pemmican as last night—we pretend to prefer the pemmican this way. Marched for 5 hours this morning over a slightly better surface covered with high moundy sastrugi. Sledge capsized twice; we pulled on foot, covering about 5½ miles. We are two pony marches and 4 miles about from our depôt. Our fuel dreadfully low and the poor Soldier nearly done. It is pathetic enough because we can do nothing for him; more hot food might do a little, but only a little, I fear. We none of us expected these terribly low temperatures, and of the rest of us Wilson is feeling them most; mainly, I fear, from his self-sacrificing devotion in doctoring Oates' feet. We cannot help each other, each has enough to do to take care of himself. We get cold on the march when the trudging is heavy, and the wind pierces our worn garments. The others, all of them, are unendingly cheerful when in the tent. We mean to see the game through with a proper spirit, but it's tough work to be pulling harder than we ever pulled in our lives for long hours, and to feel that the progress is so slow. One can only say 'God help us!' and plod on our weary way, cold and very miserable, though outwardly cheerful. We talk of all sorts of subjects in the tent, not much of food now, since we decided to take the risk of running a full ration. We simply couldn't go hungry at this time.

*Wednesday, March 7.*—A little worse, I fear. One of Oates' feet *very* bad this morning; he is wonderfully brave. We still talk of what we will do together at home.

We only made 6½ miles yesterday. This morning in 4½ hours we did just over 4 miles. We are 16 from our depôt. If we only find the correct proportion of food there and this surface continues, we may get to the next depôt [Mt. Hooper, 72 miles farther] but not to One Ton Camp. We hope against hope that the dogs have been to Mt. Hooper; then we might pull through. If there is a shortage of oil again we can have little hope. One feels that for poor Oates the crisis is near, but none of us are improving, though we are wonderfully fit considering the really excessive work we are doing. We are only kept going by good food. No wind this morning till a chill northerly air came ahead. Sun bright and cairns showing up well. I should like to keep the track to the end.

*Thursday, March 8.*—Lunch. Worse and worse in morning; poor Oates' left foot can never last out, and time over foot-gear something awful. Have to wait in night foot-gear for nearly an hour before I start changing, and then am generally first to be ready. Wilson's feet giving trouble now. We did 4½ miles this morning and are now 8½ miles from the depôt—a ridiculously small distance to feel in difficulties, yet on this surface we know we cannot equal half our old marches, and that for that effort we expend nearly double the energy. The great question is, What shall we find at the depôt? If the dogs have visited it we may get along a good distance, but if there is another short allowance of fuel, God help us indeed. We are in a very bad way, I fear, in any case.

*Saturday, March 10.*—Things steadily downhill. Oates' foot worse. He has rare pluck and must know that he can never get through. He asked Wilson if he had a chance this morning, and of course Bill had to say he didn't know. In point of fact he has none. Apart from him, if he went under now, I doubt whether we could get through. With great care we might have a dog's chance, but no more. The weather conditions are awful, and our gear gets steadily more icy and difficult to manage. At the same time, of course, poor Titus is the greatest handicap. He keeps us waiting in the morning until we have partly lost the warming effect of our good breakfast, when the only wise policy is to be up and away at once; again at lunch. Poor chap! it is too pathetic to watch him; one cannot but try to cheer him up.

Yesterday we marched up the depôt, Mt. Hooper. Cold comfort. Shortage on our allowance all round.

This morning it was calm when we breakfasted, but the wind came from the W.N.W. as we broke camp. It rapidly grew in strength. After travelling for half an hour I saw that none of us could go on facing such conditions. We were forced to camp and are spending the rest of the day in a comfortless blizzard camp, wind quite foul. [R. 52.]

*Sunday, March 11.*—Titus Oates is very near the end, one feels. What we or he will do, God only knows. We discussed the matter after breakfast; he is a brave fine fellow and understands the situation, but he practically asked for advice. Nothing could be said but to urge him to march as long as he could. One satisfactory result to the discussion; I practically ordered Wilson to hand over the means of ending our troubles to us, so that any one of us may know how to do so. Wilson had no choice between doing so and our ransacking the medicine case. We have 30 opium tabloids apiece and he is left with a tube of morphine. So far the tragical side of our story.

The sky was completely overcast when we started this morning. We could see nothing, lost the tracks, and doubtless have been swaying a good deal since—3·1 miles for the forenoon—terribly heavy dragging—expected it. Know that 6 miles is about the limit of our endurance now, if we get no help from wind or surfaces. We have 7 days' food and should be about 55 miles from One Ton Camp to-night, $6 \times 7 = 42$, leaving us 13 miles short of our distance, even if things get no worse. Meanwhile the season rapidly advances.

*Monday, March 12.*—We did 6·9 miles yesterday, under our necessary average. Things are left much the same, Oates not pulling much, and now with hands as well as feet pretty well useless. We did 4 miles this morning in 4 hours 20 min.—we may hope for 3 this afternoon, $7 \times 6 = 42$. We shall be 47 miles from the depôt. I doubt if we can possibly do it. The surface remains awful, the cold intense, and our physical condition running down.

God help us! Not a breath of favourable wind for more than a week, and apparently [we are] liable to head winds at any moment.

*Wednesday, March 14.*—No doubt about the going downhill, but everything going wrong for us. Yesterday we woke to a strong northerly wind with temp. − 37°. Couldn't face it, so remained in camp till 2, then did 5¼ miles. Wanted to march later, but party feeling the cold badly as the breeze (N.) never took off entirely, and as the sun sank the temp. fell. Long time getting supper in dark.

This morning started with southerly breeze, set sail and passed another cairn at good speed; half-way, however, the wind shifted to W. by S. or W.S.W., blew through our wind clothes and into our mits. Poor Wilson horribly cold, could [not] get off ski for some time. Bowers and I practically made camp, and when we got into the tent at last we were all deadly cold. Then temp. now midday down − 43° and the wind strong. We *must* go on, but now the making of every camp must be more difficult and dangerous. It must be near the end, but a pretty merciful end. Poor Oates got it again in the foot. I shudder to think what it will be like to-morrow. It is only with greatest pains rest of us keep off frostbites. No idea there could be temperatures like this at this time of year with such winds. Truly awful outside the tent. Must fight it out to the last biscuit, but can't reduce rations.

*Friday, March 16, or Saturday 17.*—Lost track of dates, but think the last correct. Tragedy all along the line. At lunch, the day before yesterday, poor Titus Oates said he couldn't go on; he proposed we should leave him in his sleeping-bag. That we could not do, and we induced him to come on, on the afternoon march. In spite of its awful nature for him he struggled on and we made a few miles. At night he was worse and we knew the end had come.

Should this be found I want these facts recorded. Oates' last thoughts were of his Mother, but immediately before he took pride in thinking that his regiment would be pleased with the bold way in which he met his death. We can testify to his bravery. He has borne intense suffering for weeks without complaint, and to the very last was able and willing to discuss outside subjects. He did not—would not —give up hope till the very end. He was a brave soul. This was the end. He slept through the night before last, hoping not to wake; but he woke in the morning—yesterday. It was blowing a blizzard. He said, 'I am just going outside and may be some time.' He went out into the blizzard and we have not seen him since.

I take this opportunity of saying that we have stuck to our sick companions to the last. In case of Edgar Evans, when absolutely out of food and he lay insensible, the safety of the remainder seemed to demand his abandonment, but Providence mercifully removed him at this critical moment. He died a natural death, and we did not leave him till two hours after his death. We knew that poor Oates was walking to his death, but though we tried to dissuade him, we knew it was the act of a brave man and an English gentleman. We all hope to meet the end with a similar spirit, and assuredly the end is not far.

I can only write at lunch and then only occasionally. The cold is intense, −40° at midday. My companions are unendingly cheerful, but we are all on the verge of serious frostbites, and though we constantly talk of fetching through, I don't think any one of us believes it in his heart.

We are cold on the march now, and at all times except meals. Yesterday we had to lie up for a blizzard and to-day we move dreadfully slowly. We are at No. 14 pony camp, only two pony marches from One Ton Depôt. We leave here our theodolite, a camera, and Oates' sleeping-bags. Diaries, etc., and geological specimens carried at Wilson's special request, will be found with us or on our sledge.

*Sunday, March 18.*—To-day, lunch, we are 21 miles from the depôt. Ill fortune presses, but better may come. We have had more wind and drift from ahead yesterday; had to stop marching; wind N.W., force 4, temp. −35°. No human being could face it, and we are worn out *nearly*.

My right foot has gone, nearly all the toes—two days ago I was proud possessor of best feet. These are the steps of my downfall. Like an ass I mixed a small spoonful of curry powder with my melted pemmican—it gave me violent indigestion. I lay awake and in pain all night; woke and felt done on the march; foot went and I didn't know it. A very small measure of neglect and I have a foot which is not pleasant to contemplate. Bowers takes first place in condition, but there is not much to choose after all. The others are still confident of getting through—or pretend to be—I don't know! We have the last *half* fill of oil in our primus and a very small quantity of spirit—this alone between us and thirst. The wind is fair for the moment, and that is perhaps a fact to help. The mileage would have seemed ridiculously small on our outward journey.

*Monday, March 19.*—Lunch. We camped with difficulty last night and were dreadfully cold till after our supper of cold pemmican and biscuit and a half a pannikin of cocoa cooked over the spirit. Then, contrary to expectation, we got warm and all slept well. To-day we started in the usual dragging manner. Sledge dreadfully heavy. We are 15½ miles from the depôt and ought to get there in three days. What progress! We have two days' food, but barely a day's fuel. All our feet are getting bad—Wilson's best, my right foot worse, left all right. There is no chance to nurse one's feet till we can get hot food into us. Amputation is the least I can hope for now, but will the trouble spread? That is the serious question. The weather doesn't give us a chance —the wind from N. to N.W. and − 40° temp. to-day.

*Wednesday, March 21.*—Got within 11 miles of depôt Monday night;* had to lie up all yesterday in severe blizzard. To-day forlorn hope, Wilson and Bowers going to depôt for fuel.

*22 and 23.*—Blizzard bad as ever—Wilson and Bowers unable to start—to-morrow last chance—no fuel and only one or two† of food left—must be near the end. Have decided it shall be natural—we shall march for the depôt with or without our effects and die in our tracks.

*[Thursday] March 29.*—Since the 21st we have had a continuous gale from W.S.W. and S.W. We had fuel to make two cups of tea apiece and bare food for two days on the 20th. Every day we have been ready to start for our depôt 11 *miles* away, but outside the door of the tent it remains a scene of whirling drift. I do not think we can hope for any better things now. We shall stick it out to the end, but we are getting weaker, of course, and the end cannot be far.

It seems a pity, but I do not think I can write more.

R. SCOTT.

Last entry. For God's sake look after our people.

* The 60th camp from the Pole.
† Word missing: evidently 'rations.'

we shall stick it out
to the end but we
are getting weaker of
course and the end
cannot be far.

It seems a pity but
I do not think I can
write more —

R. Scott

Last Entry —

For God's sake look
after our people

Facsimile of the last page of the journal

Scott, wearing the wallet in which he carried his sledging journals

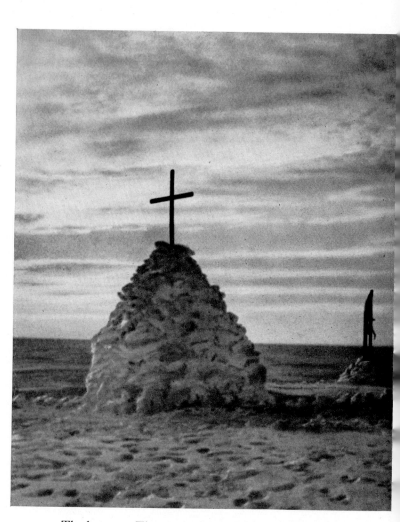

The last rest. The grave of Scott, Wilson and Bowers

With the diaries in the tent were found letters, from which come the following extracts:

The Great God has called me and I feel it will add a fearful blow to the heavy ones that have fallen on you in life. But take comfort in that I die at peace with the world and myself—not afraid.

Indeed it has been most singularly unfortunate, for the risks I have taken never seemed excessive.

. . . I want to tell you that we have missed getting through by a narrow margin which was justifiably within the risk of such a journey. . . . After all, we have given our lives for our country—we have actually made the longest journey on record, and we have been the first Englishmen at the South Pole.

You must understand that it is too cold to write much.

. . . It's a pity the luck doesn't come our way, because every detail of equipment is right.

I shall not have suffered any pain, but leave the world fresh from harness and full of good health and vigour.

Since writing the above we got to within 11 miles of our depôt, with one hot meal and two days' cold food. We should have got through but have been held for *four* days by a frightful storm. I think the best chance has gone. We have decided not to kill ourselves, but to fight to the last for that depôt, but in the fighting there is a painless end.

Make the boy* interested in natural history if you can; it is better than games; they encourage it at some schools. I know you will keep him in the open air.

Above all, he must guard and you must guard him against indolence. Make him a strenuous man. I had to force

* His son Peter.

12

myself into being strenuous, as you know—had always an inclination to be idle.

There is a piece of the Union Jack I put up at the South Pole in my private kit bag, together with Amundsen's black flag and other trifles. Send a small piece of the Union Jack to the King and a small piece to Queen Alexandra.

What lots and lots I could tell you of this journey! How much better has it been than lounging in too great comfort at home! What tales you would have for the boy! But what a price to pay!

Tell Sir Clements I thought much of him and never regretted his putting me in command of the *Discovery*.

If this letter reaches you, Bill [Dr. Wilson] and I will have gone out together. We are very near it now and I should like you to know how splendid he was at the end—everlastingly cheerful and ready to sacrifice himself for others, never a word of blame to me for leading him into this mess. He is not suffering, luckily, at least only minor discomforts.

His eyes have a comfortable blue look of hope and his mind is peaceful with the satisfaction of his faith in regarding himself as part of the great scheme of the Almighty. I can do no more to comfort you than to tell you that he died as he lived, a brave, true man—the best of comrades and staunchest of friends.

My whole heart goes out to you in pity. . . .

I am afraid this will reach you after one of the heaviest blows of your life.

I write when we are very near the end of our journey, and I am finishing it in company with two gallant, noble gentlemen. One of these is your son [Lt. Bowers]. He had come to be one of my closest and soundest friends, and I appreciate his wonderful upright nature, his ability and energy. As the troubles have thickened his dauntless spirit ever shone brighter and he has remained cheerful, hopeful, and indomitable to the end.

The ways of Providence are inscrutable, but there must be some reason why such a young, vigorous, and promising life is taken.

To the end he has talked of you and his sisters. One sees what a happy home he must have had, and perhaps it is well to look back on nothing but happiness.

He remains unselfish, self-reliant and splendidly hopeful to the end, believing in God's mercy to you. . . .

We are showing that Englishmen can still die with a bold spirit, fighting it out to the end. It will be known that we have accomplished our object in reaching the Pole, and that we have done everything possible, even to sacrificing ourselves in order to save sick companions. I think this makes an example for Englishmen of the future, and that the country ought to help those who are left behind to mourn us. I leave my poor girl and your godson, Wilson leaves a widow, and Edgar Evans also a widow in humble circumstances. Do what you can to get their claims recognised. Good-bye. I am not at all afraid of the end, but sad to miss many a humble pleasure which I had planned for the future on our long marches. I may not have proved a great explorer, but we have done the greatest march ever made and come very near to great success. . . . We are in a desperate state, feet frozen, etc. No fuel and a long way from food, but it would do your heart good to be in our tent, to hear our songs and the cheery conversation as to what we will do when we get to Hut Point.

*Later.*—We are very near the end, but have not and will not lose our good cheer. We have had four days of storm in our tent and nowhere's food or fuel. We did intend to finish ourselves when things proved like this, but we have decided to die naturally in the track.

As a dying man, my dear friend, be good to my wife and child. Give the boy a chance in life if the State won't do it. He ought to have good stuff in him. . . . I never met a man in my life whom I admired and loved more than you [Sir J. M. Barrie], but I could never show you how much your friendship meant to me, for you had much to give and I nothing.

I fear we have shot our bolt—but we have been to the Pole and done the longest journey on record.

I hope these letters may find their destination some day.

Subsidiary reasons of our failure to return are due to the sickness of different members of the party, but the real thing that has stopped us is the awful weather and un-expected cold towards the end of the journey.

This traverse of the Barrier has been quite three times as severe as any experience we had on the summit.

There is no accounting for it, but the result has thrown out my calculations, and here we are little more than 100 miles from the base and petering out.

# 16

# The Finding of the Dead

(By Lieut. Atkinson, R.N.)

EIGHT months afterwards we found the tent. It was an object partially snowed up and looking like a cairn. Before it were the ski sticks and in front of them a bamboo which probably was the mast of the sledge. The tent was practically on the line of cairns which we had built in the previous season. It was within a quarter of a mile of the remains of the cairn, which showed as a small hummock beneath the snow.

Inside the tent were the bodies of Captain Scott, Doctor Wilson, and Lieutenant Bowers. Wilson and Bowers were found in the attitude of sleep, their sleeping-bags closed over their heads as they would naturally close them.

Scott died later. He had thrown back the flaps of his sleeping-bag and opened his coat. The little wallet containing the three notebooks was under his shoulders, and his arm was flung across Wilson. They had pitched their tent well, and it had withstood all the blizzards of an exceptionally hard winter. Each man of the Expedition recognised the bodies. From Captain Scott's diary I found his reasons for this disaster. When the men had been assembled I read to them these reasons, the place of death of Petty Officer Evans, and the story of Captain Oates' heroic end.

We recovered all their gear and dug out the sledge with their belongings on it. Amongst these were 35 lbs. of very important geological specimens which had been collected on the moraines of the Beardmore Glacier; at Doctor Wilson's request they had stuck to these up to the very end, even when disaster stared them in the face and they knew that the specimens were so much weight added to what they had to pull.

When everything had been gathered up, we covered them with the outer tent and read the Burial Service. From this time until well into the next day we started to build a mighty cairn above them. This cairn was finished the next morning, and upon it a rough cross was placed, made from the greater portion of two skis, and on either side were up-ended two sledges, and they were fixed firmly in the snow, to be an added mark. Between the eastern sledge and the cairn a bamboo was placed, containing a metal cylinder, and in this the following record was left:—

'November 12, 1912, lat. 79 degrees, 50 mins. South. This cross and cairn are erected over the bodies of Captain Scott, C.V.O., R.N., Doctor E. A. Wilson, M.B., B.C. Cantab., and Lieutenant H. R. Bowers, Royal Indian Marine—a slight token to perpetuate their successful and gallant attempt to reach the Pole. This they did on January 17, 1912, after the Norwegian Expedition had already done so. Inclement weather with lack of fuel was the cause of their death. Also to commemorate their two gallant comrades, Captain L. E. G. Oates of the Inniskilling Dragoons, who walked to his death in a blizzard to save his comrades about eighteen miles south of this position; also of Seaman Edgar Evans, who died at the foot of the

Beardmore Glacier. "The Lord gave and the Lord taketh away; blessed be the name of the Lord.""

This was signed by all the members of the party. I decided then to march twenty miles south with the whole of the Expedition and try to find the body of Captain Oates.

For half that day we proceeded south, as far as possible along the line of the previous season's march. On one of the old pony walls, which was simply marked by a ridge of the surface of the snow, we found Oates' sleeping-bag, which they had brought along with them after he had left.

The next day we proceeded thirteen more miles south, hoping and searching to find his body. When we arrived at the place where he had left them, we saw that there was no chance of doing so. The kindly snow had covered his body, giving him a fitting burial. Here, again, as near to the site of the death as we could judge, we built another cairn to his memory, and placed thereon a small cross and the following record:

'Hereabouts died a very gallant gentleman, Captain L. E. G. Oates of the Inniskilling Dragoons. In March 1912, returning from the Pole, he walked willingly to his death in a blizzard, to try and save his comrades, beset by hardships. This note is left by the Relief Expedition of 1912.'

It was signed by Cherry-Garrard and myself.

On the second day we came again to the resting-place of the three and bade them a final farewell. There alone in their greatness they will lie without change or bodily decay, with the most fitting tomb in the world above them.

In the following January, when the *Terra Nova* returned for the last time to bring the survivors home, those who had taken part in the search for Captain Scott sledged out to Hut Point to erect a cross in memory of him and his companions.

This cross, 9 feet in height, which was made by Davies of Australian jarrah wood, now stands on the summit of Observation Hill, overlooking the Great Ice Barrier and in full view of the *Discovery* winter quarters.

The line chosen from Tennyson's 'Ulysses' was suggested by Cherry-Garrard.

IN
MEMORIAM
CAPT. R. F. SCOTT, R.N.
DR. E. A. WILSON, CAPT. L. E. G. OATES, INS. DRGS.,
LT. H. R. BOWERS, R.I.M.
PETTY OFFICER E. EVANS, R.N.
WHO DIED ON THEIR
RETURN FROM THE
POLE, MARCH
1912.
TO STRIVE, TO SEEK,
TO FIND,
AND NOT TO
YIELD.

# Message to the Public

THE causes of the disaster are not due to faulty organisation, but to misfortune in all risks which had to be undertaken.

1. The loss of pony transport in March 1911 obliged me to start later than I had intended, and obliged the limits of stuff transported to be narrowed.

2. The weather throughout the outward journey, and especially the long gale in 83° S., stopped us.

3. The soft snow in lower reaches of glacier again reduced pace.

We fought these untoward events with a will and conquered, but it cut into our provision reserve.

Every detail of our food supplies, clothing and depôts made on the interior ice-sheet and over that long stretch of 700 miles to the Pole and back, worked out to perfection. The advance party would have returned to the glacier in fine form and with surplus of food, but for the astonishing failure of the man whom we had least expected to fail. Edgar Evans was thought the strongest man of the party.

The Beardmore Glacier is not difficult in fine weather, but on our return we did not get a single completely fine day; this with a sick companion enormously increased our anxieties.

As I have said elsewhere, we got into frightfully rough ice and Edgar Evans received a concussion of the brain— he died a natural death, but left us a shaken party with the season unduly advanced.

But all the facts above enumerated were as nothing to

the surprise which awaited us on the Barrier. I maintain that our arrangements for returning were quite adequate, and that no one in the world would have expected the temperatures and surfaces which we encountered at this time of the year. On the summit in lat. 85°, 86° we had −20°, −30°. On the Barrier in lat 82°, 10,000 feet lower, we had −30° in the day, −47° at night pretty regularly, with continuous head wind during our day marches. It is clear that these circumstances came on very suddenly, and our wreck is certainly due to this sudden advent of severe weather, which does not seem to have any satisfactory cause. I do not think human beings ever came through such a month as we have come through, and we should have got through in spite of the weather but for the sickening of a second companion, Captain Oates, and a shortage of fuel in our depôts for which I cannot account,* and finally, but for the storm which has fallen on us within 11 miles of the depôt at which we hoped to secure our final supplies. Surely misfortune could scarcely have exceeded this last blow. We arrived within 11 miles of our old One Ton Camp with fuel for one last meal and food for two days. For four† days we have been unable to leave the tent—the gale howling about us. We are weak, writing is difficult, but for my own sake I do not regret this journey, which has shown that Englishmen can endure hardships, help one another, and meet death with as great a fortitude as ever in the past. We took risks, we knew we took them; things have come out against us, and therefore we have no cause for complaint, but bow to the will of Providence, determined still to do our best to the last. But if we have been willing to give our

* There is no doubt that it had evaporated.
† They actually lasted six more days after this!

lives to this enterprise, which is for the honour of our country, I appeal to our countrymen to see that those who depend on us are properly cared for.

Had we lived, I should have had a tale to tell of the hardi-hood, endurance, and courage of my companions which would have stirred the heart of every Englishman. These rough notes and our dead bodies must tell the tale, but surely, surely, a great rich country like ours will see that those who are dependent on us are properly provided for.

R. SCOTT